Virginia Woolf & Vanessa Bell
A CHILDHOOD IN ST IVES

Marion Whybrow

First published in Great Britain in 2014
Reprinted 2018

Copyright © 2014 Marion Whybrow

All rights reserved. No part of this publication may be
reproduced, stored in a retrieval system, or transmitted in
any form or by any means without the prior permission
of the copyright holder.

British Library Cataloguing-in-Publication Data
A CIP record for this title is available from the British Library

ISBN 978 1 906690 57 1

HALSTAR
Halsgrove House,
Ryelands Business Park,
Bagley Road, Wellington, Somerset TA21 9PZ
Tel: 01823 653777   Fax: 01823 216796
email: sales@halsgrove.com

Part of the Halsgrove group of companies
Information on all Halsgrove titles is available at: www.halsgrove.com

Printed in India by Parksons Graphics

Contents

Acknowledgements	4
Author's Preface	5
Foreword by Helen Dunmore	7
INTRODUCTION TO ST IVES	9
VIRGINIA WOOLF	33
VANESSA BELL	79
Brief Chronology	121
References	122
Select Bibliography	125
Index	127

Acknowledgements

My husband Terry for all his belief, support and reading the script.
My daughter Kim, for her careful reading of the script.
Helen Dunmore for her Foreword.
Jennie Hancox for maps.

Thanks for help, photos and permissions

Janet Axten, Anne Olivier Bell, Barbara Blumenthal, Lena and Donald Bray, Libraries and Museums, Brighton, Judie Browne, Jane Burnett, Simon Butler and Sharon O'Inn at Halsgrove, Dick Chapman and Ben Duncan, Kathleen Coleman, Anthony Curtis, Marion Dell, Helen Dunmore, Henrietta Garnett for images © Estate of Vanessa Bell, Hogarth Press, Chris Hibbert, Jonathan Holmes, Ann Kelley, kernowphoto, Kim Lynch, Brian Pierce, Montpelier Gallery, Mortimer Rare Book Room, Smith College USA, National Portrait Gallery, National Trust Photo Library, Oxford University Press, Joan Ralph, Random House Group, Belinda Ratnayake, The Society of Authors, Stephen family descendants, St Ives Archive, St Ives Arts Club, St Ives Library, St Ives Museum (Comley Collection), Richard Shone, Liz Shore, Slade School of Fine Art, Brian and Margaret Stevens, Tate Gallery, David Tovey, Vimlan, Sheila Wilkinson, Greta Williams.

Author's Preface

It is in our idleness, in our dreams,
that the submerged truth sometimes comes to the top.[1]

The most important memory in Virginia Woolf's childhood in St Ives was of lying in bed 'half awake, half asleep,' in the nursery at Talland House. 'It is of hearing the waves breaking, one, two, one, two, and sending a splash of water over the beach.' Vanessa also had her revelatory moments but Virginia expressed these innermost cerebral memories for both of them. Vanessa's visual eye recorded what she saw and her approach was pragmatic and matter of fact; 'no family member could share with Vanessa her longing to paint.'

As Vanessa grew older in those long summers of childhood by the sea, her natural eye for colour, shape and form developed. St Ives, with its plethora of artists and studios, its writers and the Arts Club, was a good breeding ground for the talents of two young creative minds.

In Virginia's book, *Moments of Being* we discover those intimate details of her thoughts and revelations about what has moved her, what has influenced her, what has been instrumental in forming her ideas for future inclusion in her various books. We understand the intensity of her feelings and experiences. The sisters were so united in their endeavours in pursuing their purpose in life, to become a writer and a painter, that they mirrored each other, sharing a common family experience but forming between the two of them 'a very close conspiracy'.

Marion Whybrow
St Ives, 2014

Foreword by Helen Dunmore

Childhood is a repository of images on which the human being will draw for the rest of his or her life. Marion Whybrow looks back from the formidable artists in words and paint that Virginia Woolf and Vanessa Bell became, to the children they once were. Her argument about the potent role of St Ives in the sisters' lives and creative development is a compelling one. It takes us to Talland House in its two or three acres of garden above Porthminster Beach: here the Stephen family spent long summers from 1881 to 1895. Virginia and Vanessa learned to play cricket, swim, boat, tramp across country, hunt moths, fish in rockpools and discover the unique character of this little town on the edge of the Atlantic.

The family arrived in St Ives for several months each summer. During those formative years, Vanessa and Virginia Stephen had two homes and two lives, and it's arguable that their St Ives life left the deeper impression. Without those early years by the sea, and the sounds and images laid down in brain and senses, Woolf would have been a different writer. It is hard to imagine Virginia Woolf's fiction without the St Ives childhood memories which shaped *To The Lighthouse*, *The Waves*, and to a certain extent *Jacob's Room*.

The influence on Vanessa Bell is harder to gauge. She left less direct evidence in her painting than Woolf did in her writing. However, Marion Whybrow offers evidence that Vanessa Bell's early experience of St Ives' rich artistic life was a powerful influence on her. Here, painting was an everyday thing. Vanessa Bell saw artists at work on the beaches, in the lanes, or on Smeaton's Pier. Newlyn and St Ives were not artistic backwaters. Artists here were in the forefront of new approaches to painting, and they knew it.

Through family friendships in St Ives and through the St Ives Arts Club, Vanessa encountered artists such as Adrian Stokes, Louis Grier and Stanhope Forbes. She visited studios, attended exhibitions and began her own long apprenticeship in drawing and painting. Vanessa might also have observed that there were women, including Elizabeth Stanhope Forbes and Helene Schjerfbeck, among the painters whose work was exhibited and admired.

It's summer. Talland House is packed with visitors, and resounds with the quarrels and alliances of a large family. The father, Leslie Stephen, is theatrically emotional and demanding. Two girls slip away to the attic –

'as stealthily as stags' – to talk about what they want to do with their lives. Each discovers that she has a vocation: one to write, the other to paint.

There will be many obstacles and delays, but what is striking is that these two Victorian girls should conceive such ambitions. Their family did not encourage women to enter professions. Women should be beautiful, charitable, charming promoters of male achievement rather than the realisers of their own dreams.

It may be that the physical freedom of their St Ives life helped these sisters to conceive of independence. Their winter life in London was constricted by decorum and chaperonage, but in St Ives there was the large garden with its path running down to the beach, day-long rambles in the wild countryside of West Penwith, and explorations of the intricate, salty little fishing town. Even within the house, doors were open to the sun and the salt breeze. The opposed values of London and St Ives foreshadowed the battle which these girls would later fight and win, by going off to live in Bloomsbury as writer and artist.

Talland House in the 1880s and early 1890s possessed a loveliness of setting and an atmosphere which haunted both Virginia Woolf and Vanessa Bell throughout their lives. Bell described in a letter her overwhelming emotion on first reading *To the Lighthouse* and recognising that her sister, like the fictional painter Lily Briscoe in the novel, had created from their shared childhood a modernist work of art which revealed inner truth as well as outer appearance.

When the sisters were thirteen and fifteen, their mother died and the lease on Talland House was given up. Their childhood was over, and the transition to adulthood was hard. St Ives might have become merely a source of unhappy longing and nostalgia, but Virginia Woolf and Vanessa Bell were tougher than that. They held on to the childhood images within them, as they held on to their ambitions. Slowly, garden, lighthouse, the blaze of summer, a mother knitting and a blind-cord tapping were translated into the greatest of art.

Helen Dunmore

An Introduction to St Ives

St Ives: a town on the 'very toe-nail of England'

"The town was then much as it must have been in the sixteenth century: a scramble, a pyramid, of whitewashed granite houses, crusting the slope made in the hollow under the Island. It was built there for shelter – built for a few fishermen, when Cornwall was a country more remote from England than Spain is now. It was a steep little town. Many houses had stairs running up from the pavement to the door. The walls were thick blocks of granite, to stand the sea and gales, I suppose. They were splashed with a wash the colour of Cornish cream. There was nothing mellow about them. There was no red brick: there was no thatch; the eighteenth century had left no mark, as it has in the south. St Ives might have been built yesterday; or in the time of the Conqueror. It had no architecture; no conscious arrangement. The market place was a jagged cobbled open place; the Church was a granite church – of what age, I do not know. It was a windy, noisy, fishy, vociferous, narrow-streeted town; the colour of a mussel or a limpet; like a bunch of rough shell fish, oysters, or mussels, all crowded together."[1]

St Ives Harbour

Discovering St Ives

St Ives was discovered by Leslie Stephen on a walking tour of Cornwall. Its population relied on the fishing industry. Its harbour, in the days of pilchard fishing and processing, was the hub of activity, with its seine boats, fish auctions, and horse and carts to transport salted and pressed barrels of pilchards from the harbour. There were boat builders along the sandy foreshore, where new boats were launched into the sea, direct from the workshop. Cornish luggers and seine boats for catching pilchards filled the bowl of the harbour, with their huge canvas sails, dwarfing the tiny cottages Men, women and children were involved in the work, which supported their daily lives.

Fishermen and mackerel fleet
St Ives Harbour 1890s

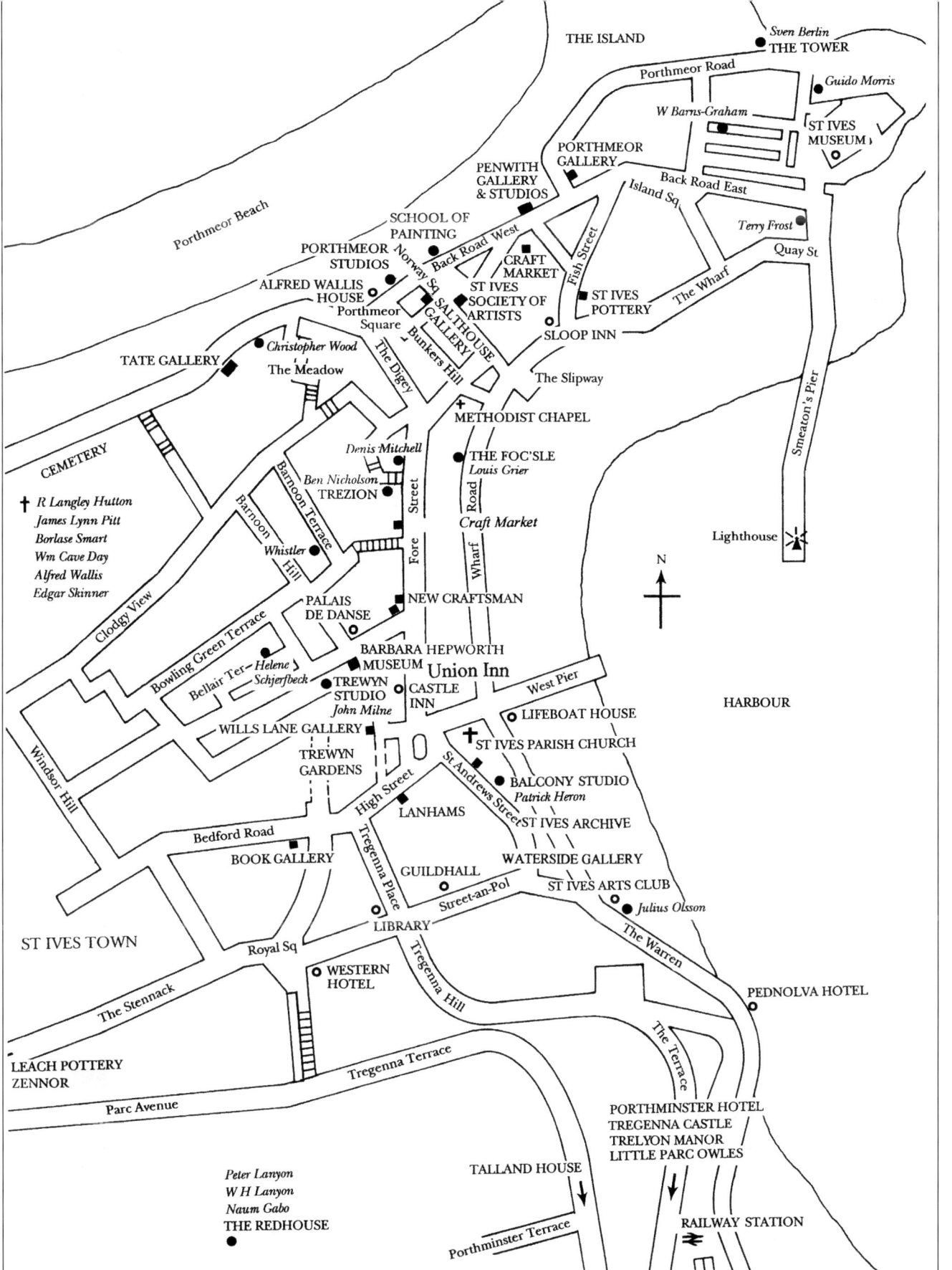

Talland House 2012 with the Edward Hain Hospital far left

Talland House 1880s

Talland House and the children's favourite Porthminster Beach

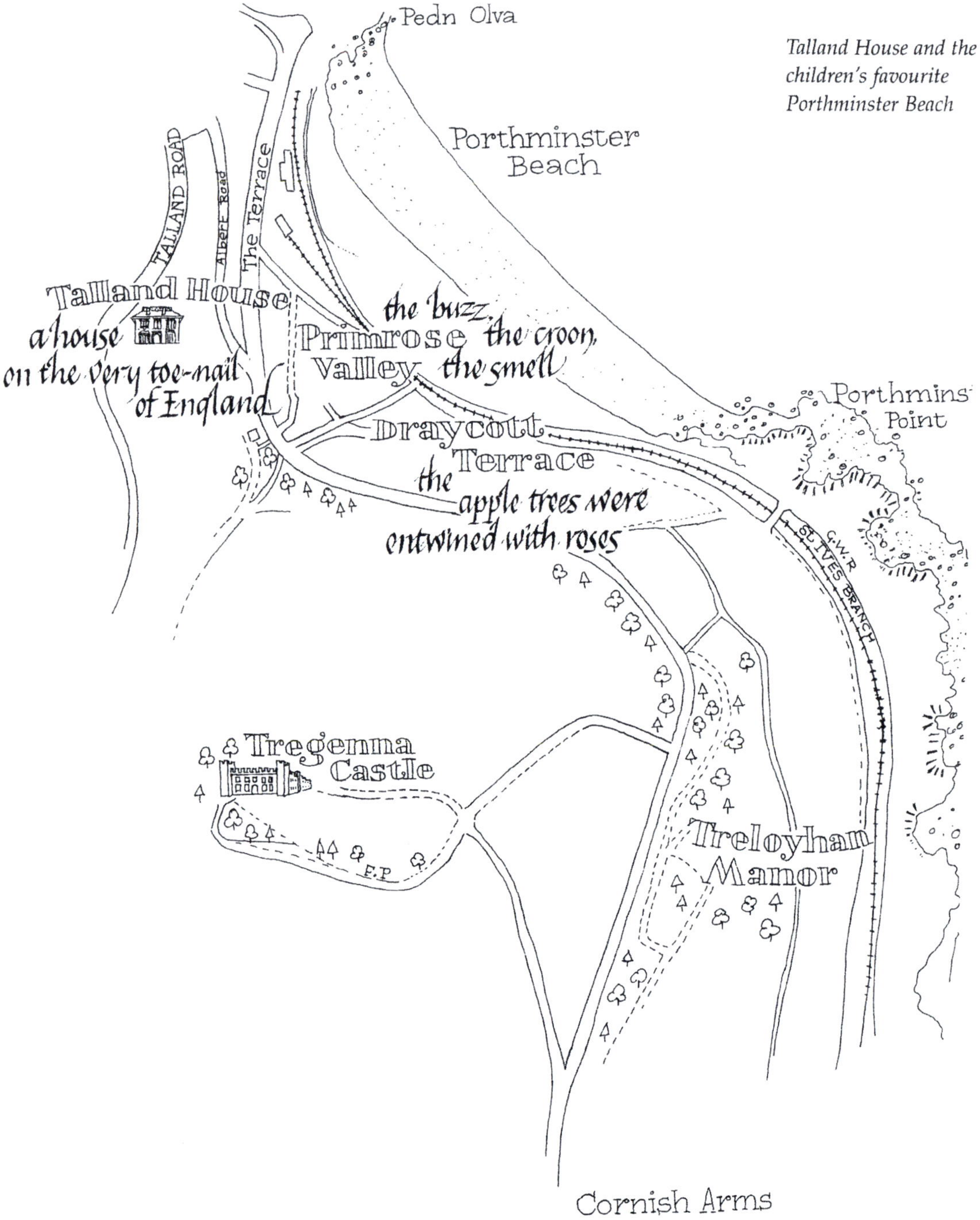

Talland House and Porthminster Beach

AN INTRODUCTION TO ST IVES

Buying Talland House

Leslie and Julia Stephen bought the lease of Talland House in this working town in 1881. From this permanent base the family could explore the area west of St Ives towards Land's End and walk into an ancient landscape untouched by farming; revealing prehistoric sites, hut circles, ancient barrows and quoits. There was an abundance of wild flowers and untried sea cliffs to climb. For several months each year St Ives became the haven for the children, Vanessa, Thoby, Virginia and Adrian.

The two lighthouses on Smeaton's Pier

Downalong

St Ives is a small town built on sand at the edge of two seas, between the safe haven of the harbour and the threatening Atlantic ocean sweeping the rocky coast on the sixteen mile journey to Land's End. Smeaton's pier, built in 1770, protecting the harbour, has a stone-built lighthouse with a viewing gallery round the top. The building of an extension to the pier, with its second octagonal iron-clad lighthouse, was completed in 1890. The Stephen family, who stayed in the town over a period of thirteen years, must have witnessed the building of this additional lighthouse and quay on their annual holidays. West Pier was added in 1894.

West Pier by Arnesby Brown RA, 1908

The cottages are made of local building materials, Cornish Delabole slate and granite. Narrow cobblestone lanes separate the houses, fish cellars, and net lofts.

Virginia Woolf & Vanessa Bell - A CHILDHOOD IN ST IVES

High Street, St Ives c.1900

High Street 2014

AN INTRODUCTION TO ST IVES

Upalong

The Stephens' family home was above the working town, where the gentry lived and built their houses. Talland House was an elegant building, surrounded by spacious grounds. Its balconied windows overlooked the great expanse of water of St Ives Bay, out to Godrevy lighthouse and beyond.

The four younger children would spend up to three months every year, in their ideal home, accompanied by Mr and Mrs Stephen and Stella who, in August 1893 at the age of twenty-four, wrote in her diary: '*Ginia, Thoby & Adrian went off to fish (caught nothing!) Father botanised. Mother went round of Roaches, Crays etc. Nessa & I sat in garden, she painted I worked – cricket with Dick as usual.*' [2]

There was a good supply of servants in the town, as well as the local tradespeople, who brought provisions and services daily. Although the Stephen family arrived with their own servants to Talland House, they still employed local gardeners and a housekeeper to maintain the premises in their absence. With such a large household, and a host of visitors, local provisions were in great demand and the town began to flourish.

At the end of one particular holiday at Talland House, Stella recorded the Stephen family's departure. *Left St Ives. A large party. Lisa, Georgie 3 ch*[ildren]. *& 4 servants. 2 compartments in corridor train. Train 1 hour late. Gerald met us.*[3] [at Paddington Station]

Front entrance of Talland House

The Branch Line

For some years the Great Western Railway had served Cornwall from Paddington to Penzance, the end of the line to the West country. However, in 1877 with the building of a branch line, the steam locomotive the *Cornish Riviera* arrived at St Ives station. This produced a significant increase in the tourist trade. The station was built above Porthminster beach and the fishing boats sheltered beneath the railway bridge. In due course the boats disappeared and Victorian bathing tents gave way to wind breaks, surf-boards, and the present-day holidaymaker.

The train to St Ives travels four and a half miles along the picturesque coastline, with a view to Godrevy lighthouse and the bay; until it rounds the bend and catches the breathtaking view of St Ives harbour. People alight almost on to the fine sun-bleached sands of Porthminster beach.

St Ives Station 1900s

Present day St Ives station rail tracks, now a car park

Fishing

When Leslie and Julia Stephen brought their family to St Ives, the fishing industry was still the major source of employment. There were many family owned-boats and most cottages had their own cellar for storage of fishing gear or for pressing fish to extract the oil and brine, with a flight of stone steps leading to the living quarters.

There were seasons for catching mackerel, herring and pilchards. There was long-lining for hake, dogfish, plaice, whiting and ray. But it was the pilchard for which St Ives was best known, most of which were exported to Italy. They came into the bay in their millions. Seine boats were lined up ready at Porthminster beach awaiting the cry of 'Hevva,' from the watchful huers on a high point overlooking the bay.

The seine boats would put out and trap the pilchards in a circle of nets where they were held in a heaving mass of silver until the small boats, known as dippers, scooped up the fish and ferried them to shore.

It was from Carbis Bay that Virginia remembered hearing the sound of the huer's horn calling to the fishermen to launch the boats and 'shoot the seine.' They were rowed out into the mass of

Catch of Pilchards *by Fred Sargent, 1895*

St Ives Harbour – pilchards packed in barrels for export

Virginia Woolf & Vanessa Bell - A CHILDHOOD IN ST IVES

The Huer signalling the position of a shoal of pilchards

Dipping out pilchards from the tuck net. Porthminster 1905

silver fish and returned with some of the catch in their own small boat. Another time they watched the pilchard swarm into the bay, the seine nets were shot, but there was a misjudgement of the signals given by the huer, who was dancing in a fury as he watched the shoal move out of the bay

This lively and necessary life-maintaining fishing industry gradually declined, and by 1900 St Ives had lost much of its fleet. Large-scale fishing in West Cornwall is now centred in Newlyn.

A feature of Porthminster beach in my youth was the fleet of big, tarry seine boats drawn up on the foreshore and up the valley – three hundred of them, each with attendant tow-boats and bearing its owner's mark brightly coloured upon its black bow. [4]

Seine Boats on Porthminster Beach with old cottages and train station

Top left: St Ives lifeboat

Top right: Launching the lifeboat with a tractor

Below: The rescue helicopter in an exercise over Smeaton's Pier for Lifeboat Day

Royal National Lifeboat Institution

Playing a crucial role in the town and in the psyche of local folk, whose menfolk manned the lifeboats, was the tradition of rescuing those at sea. "The heroic spirit was born in them. The call to duty was enough."

In 1938 the St Ives Lifeboat, the Caroline Parsons, was launched to rescue the crew of a ship, *Alba* which had been heading for St Ives harbour when it hit rocks off Porthmeor beach. The crew were taken off safely but the lifeboat was hit broadside as she turned to make for the harbour. She overturned, throwing the crews of the lifeboat and the *Alba* into the sea.

Many rescues were achieved that night by people on the beach who had waded into the water to save the men. The crew of the lifeboat survived but five from the *Alba* were drowned. Two are buried in Barnoon cemetery.

In 1939 the St Ives lifeboat, *John and Sarah Eliza Stych*, put to sea to rescue a ship foundering in fierce seas off Cape Cornwall. The lifeboat got no further than Clodgy Point, off Porthmeor, when the boat capsized. It overturned several times and each time men were drowned. The lifeboat and the remainder of the crew were lost to the rocks at Godrevy save for one man, William Freeman who, as a young man, had acted as boatman to the Stephens at Talland House. He was washed up alive, injured and exhausted on the shore near Gwithian but managed to raise the alarm. William Freeman died years later on the 39th anniversary of the disaster.

AN INTRODUCTION TO ST IVES

Before a tractor came into use, eighty men launched the lifeboat, hauling it along the Wharf and down the slipway on the harbour.

Clodgy *by Sydney Mortimer Laurence 1890s*

The wreck of the *Alba* by Alfred Wallis

The Crowns, Botallack mine

Mining

Although fishing was the major occupation of St Ives, tin and copper mining played an active role in the area surrounding the town. When the fish were in short supply mining helped provide a temporary income. Mines opened and closed in quick succession. As well as deep mining, open cast mining was carried out on hillsides above the town. Rosewall Hill, which towers over St Ives, is full of the remains of dangerous and abandoned workings. All over Cornwall the ruins of engine houses rear up out of the landscape and perch on the edges of cliffs, where mine workings were tunnelled under the sea.

St Ives miners lived in nearby Halsetown, a new model village, built to house families in sturdy buildings with their own gardens, or they lived in terraced houses along the Stennack stream, which flowed down the valley to St Ives to discharge into the sea. Stennack means place of tin. In lean times many miners emigrated to South Africa, Australia and America where their skills were needed. Such was the rate of emigration that it is said that in every hole in the ground in any country, there is a Cornishman.

Drawing of miners at Geevor Mine by Borlase Smart

Giew Tin Mine St Ives

Farming

Like all rural communities, there was a great reliance on farming, which supported the fishermen and miners' families, and all folk were engaged in harvesting. Farming, mining and fishing lived side by side all the way from St Ives and West Penwith, on to Land's End.

An Edward Hain house, Folly Farm built 1901

Farming, with mine chimneys on Rosewall Hill, opposite Folly Farm

Local land owner, Edward Hain, cultivated farming and mining in the area. He built substantial houses in the parish of Towednack for his tenant farmers. They are easily recognised being of the same size and design, with five bedrooms, two reception rooms and large kitchen. There was a separate living area for a farm hand. The houses bear the initials EH above the door. The dates of the buildings range from the turn of the century and can be seen dotted around the landscape on the way to Zennor.

Close to town there were small field systems on the cliffs at Man's Head worked by St Ives folk. They grew daffodils for market and food for the family. The remains of these field patterns, with their stone hedges, can still be seen on the cliffs. Families also owned their own pig. These were kept at Porthgwidden, which is now a beautiful sandy cove favoured by families with small children.

Sir Edward Hain built his own mansion, Treloyhan Manor, in extensive grounds above the town in 1892. He was knighted for his contribution to British shipping. His fleet of ships, the Hain

AN INTRODUCTION TO ST IVES

Shipping Line with their distinctive H on the funnel were built in Hayle and registered in St Ives. In 1893 Stella Duckworth recorded in her diary, *Mother Nessa and I went to* Hain[s] *Palace. Met Mrs H coming here but went to see the Palace with her. Nice house not beautiful 14 bedrooms ... rather large for the 2 little Hains and their 3 ch*[ildren].[5] Treloyhan Manor was for many years a Christian holiday centre, but now the estate has sold land for housing development.

Man's Head *by James Lynn Pitt*

Treloyhan Manor built 1892

Lady Hain, Miss Hain and friend in St Ives

Memorial to Julia

In 1895 Julia Stephen died in London. She was 49. This ended the long, ideal, thirteen summer holidays in Cornwall. Her youngest children were Vanessa 16, Thoby 15, Virginia 13 and Adrian 12. Julia's commitment to helping the poor families in St Ives was recognized in the town and her death was mourned by many of those families who had benefitted from the attention of a trained nurse. Julia provided those services free of charge.

Leslie Stephen's memorial to his wife took the form of The Julia Prinsep Stephen Nursing Association. It was formed with the financial assistance of Leslie, the Hain family and many other friends and benefactors. Stella was appointed to the Board and Vanessa took her place after Stella's death in 1897.

In 1915 Edward Hain lost his only son in WW1 Gallipoli campaign while serving as captain with the Cornish Squadron of the Devon Yeomanry. The memorial to his son took the form of the Edward Hain Cottage Hospital set up in 1920 next door to Talland House, uniting with Julia's nursing association. Over one hundred years later The Edward Hain Hospital is loved by the townsfolk and still plays a vital role in the community.

St Ives and the Artists

St Ives is recognised as an art colony. It still flourishes today. The first artist of note to arrive was J M W Turner in 1811, who made several sketches of the town. In 1883/84 Whistler, with his pupil, Sickert were staying at Barnoon Terrace. Before the turn of the nineteenth century a large colony of artists had established itself. They were drawn by the remote area, the quality of light, the untouched rural community, the marine environment, and all the romantic ideas of artists who had travelled on the Continent to France and Brittany and found there ideal places to live and paint. They had visited the artists' colonies of Pont Aven and Concarneau in Brittany, and the two Cornish harbours of St Ives and Newlyn, just ten miles apart, reflected these ideals and offered the same facilities.

Artist Harewood Robinson noted: *Old sail lofts and cottages were sought out, and turned into studios, and large skylights appeared everywhere among the grey roofs of the old town; by the enterprise of the townspeople new studios were built, some of imposing size, and St Ives took its place as a world-known centre of art work.*[6]

The First Artists' Club

To provide for their needs, the artists set up their own societies as places to discuss and exhibit their work. The first of these was St Ives Arts Club, founded in 1890 by the artist Louis Grier who described its location: *we are in view of the glorious bay and in sound of the cry of the hovering gull, and under our feet comes the roar of the ground-sea as it struggles with the rocks at the base and rushes madly up the granite walls of our foundation. It is a very marine spot indeed.*[7]

At a meeting of the Club the secretary read a letter from Leslie Stephen, on behalf of himself and Mrs Stephen, accepting the invitation to membership. Of the hundred members they were the first to join, closely followed by Mr and Mrs Stanhope Forbes, artists from Newlyn. Mr Hain, the ship owner, and Mrs Hain were brought as guests of seascape painter Julius Olsson in this first year.

In 1891 Leslie Stephen was elected President of the Arts Club, but he did not take office because of ill health. For the same reason he was also forced to resign his editorship of the *Dictionary of National Biography,* a task which had engaged him since 1882; much of it was written in St Ives. However, that same year he was made an Honorary Doctor of Letters at Cambridge. In 1892 he was elected President of the London Library. In 1894 his literary interests were sufficient to persuade him to preside at the annual dinner of the Society of Authors.

Borlase Smart with his painting of the Arts Club

Virginia Woolf & Vanessa Bell - A CHILDHOOD IN ST IVES

Top left: A Saturday night at the Arts Club 1895

Top right: Arts Club members filming Laurence of Alaska *at Treloyhan Manor in 1989. Left. Graham Smith, Marion Whybrow, Philip Barnett, Sue Ward, actor playing Sydney Mortimer Laurence, Karen Jones, Ray Deacon, Treloyhan receptionist.*

Fishing Boats, *William Cave Day*

A Cornish Lugger, *Sydney Mortimer Laurence*

First School of Painting

Several schools of painting have flourished in the area, run by practising artists. The first was established in 1895 by Julius Olsson and Louis Grier. Their School of Landscape and Marine Painting offered, *an opportunity of studying out of door effects.* Julius Olsson, played an active role in local affairs over a period of many years. In writing of his memories years later, he stated:

There is no place in England of the size of St Ives that has had such a marked influence on the progress of British Art during the last forty years. It has been visited by so many people, distinguished in art and literature. One of my earliest recollections was dining with Leslie Stephen at Talland House. . . St Ives materially helped me in my art and I am grateful for it.[8]

Advertisements for schools stressed the importance of painting *en plein air* in the European tradition, with such artists as Algernon and Gertrude Talmage, and Charles and Ruth Simpson, who established schools for short periods. St Ives can still claim to be one of the largest art colonies, with an unbroken record from the 1880s to the present day.

Artists and Methodists

The general consensus of the townsfolk on that first influx of artists was 'Well, if they can work in the same conditions as us, they can't be too bad.' However, the living conditions of the native Cornish were harsh, with large families to raise, no indoor sanitation and typhoid still a major child killer.

However, the strict Methodist teaching prevalent at the time probably helped the women cope with their poverty and loss of children. To die was to go to heaven, a far brighter place than they would ever experience on earth.

William Holt Yates Titcomb

The artist W H Y Titcomb, friendly with a local Cornish family, visited their cottage to say goodbye before travelling to Italy to paint. On coming into the room he saw the grandmother propped up in bed, the light of ecstasy on her face. She was going to her maker. Two fishermen sons prayed, while the daughter wept at her side. Back from Italy, the artist returned to the cottage and found the old lady alive and well. Titcomb had never forgotten the scene he witnessed and persuaded the family to recreate that event in his studio.

Virginia Woolf & Vanessa Bell - A CHILDHOOD IN ST IVES

The painting *Piloting Her Home* was shown at the Royal Academy in 1894. Three large drawings of Titcomb's, hang on the walls of the Primitive Methodist Chapel in Fore Street.

Opposite: Primitive Methodists
by W H Y Titcomb 1894

Piloting Her Home
by W H Y Titcomb 1894

The Last Years

After Julia's death in 1895 Leslie's responsibilities rested heavily on him. When their mother died he did not farm his children out to various relatives as many fathers would have done and he had more than a justifiable excuse, being 63 years old.

In these last few years Leslie Stephen gained many honours from Oxford and Cambridge, Edinburgh and Harvard Universities, and several historical and antiquary societies. He was appointed a Trustee of the National Portrait Gallery. His final accolade was in 1902 when he was made a KCB, Knight Commander of the Order of the Bath.

Sir Leslie Stephen died in February 1904 aged 72. The Cornish *Western Echo*, quoting from *The Times*, described him:

The distinguished essayist and first editor of the Dictionary of National Biography died on Monday at his residence in London. He was one of the foremost men of letters of his age .. He came to fill the first place in the literary world of his day .[9]

Frederick Maitland, related to the family by marriage, wrote the first biography of Leslie Stephen in 1906 However, for Virginia and Vanessa it was time to move on from their father's Victorian mores and values and embrace the 20th century.

The Sloop Inn

The fishermen of St Ives used to meet the artists of the town in the Sloop Inn, just off the harbour slipway. Town records show that the inn has been in existence for 400 years. Many of the rafters are ships' timbers. It has been painted and photographed thousands of times. It is said that every artist who visited the town has turned up at the Sloop. One could visit the Inn to find local people and painters standing alongside their portraits or caricatures. Art exhibitions have been hosted there for a century and still take place. Visitors invariably visit the Sloop Inn to feel part of the heritage of St Ives past and present. It is a monument that unites most aspects of the town. It embraces fishermen, artists and visitors.

The Sloop Inn 1900 and 2014

Virginia Woolf

When they took Talland House, my father and mother, gave me something I think invaluable.[1]

In 1882 the Stephen family spent their first summer at Talland House, St Ives. Vanessa was three, Thoby two, Virginia not yet a year old and Adrian yet to be born. There was also older stepsister, Stella, from their mother's first marriage. The Stephen children were to enjoy thirteen years of summer holidays in Cornwall. Leslie and Julia rejoiced in having made the right decision to buy the lease. The family now had a London house in Kensington and a house by the sea.

Virginia recalls: *In retrospect, probably nothing that we had as children was quite so important to us as our summer in Cornwall . . to have our own house, our own garden – to have that bay, that sea , and the Mount: Clodgy and Halsetown bog, Carbis Bay, Lelant, Zennor, Trevail, the Gurnard's Head; to hear the waves breaking that first night behind the yellow blind; to sail in the lugger; to dig in the sand; to scramble over the rocks . . I could fill pages remembering one thing after another that made the summer at St Ives the best beginning to a life conceivable.* [2]

Virginia talks about the many aspects of the garden with its platform known as the look-out on which they would stand and watch the little coastal train arrive at St Ives station, which would often include Julia's older sons, step-brothers George and Gerald Duckworth, from their jobs in London. Talland House had lawns and orchards, kitchen gardens, a greenhouse for grapes, a cricket lawn and many play areas for four lively children when they weren't playing on the beach.

Virginia Stephen was a highly imaginative and emotional child and her early introduction to St Ives was the catalyst for her lifelong love of Cornwall. St Ives remained in her mind and in her memory and became part of her psyche. There was always a compulsion to return to this beloved place. Leonard Woolf, who married Virginia in 1912, understood this extreme passion and used it to Virginia's advantage. When she was ill and disturbed he brought her to Cornwall as the cure

Julia with Virginia on her lap

Top left: *Talland House 2014*

Top right: *Adrian, Julia, Henry James at Talland House*

for her depression and mental exhaustion, which she often experienced in the writing, or on the completion of a book.

Virginia was a productive writer and avid reader, it is surprising that she did not write poetry; words were her milieu. She grew up amidst her father's library of books and his literary, contemporary friends, who visited Leslie Stephen at their Hyde Park Gate house and those who came to Talland House. Three of those writers to visit St Ives were George Meredith 1828-1909 and three Americans, Henry James 1843-1916, John Addington Symonds 1840-1893 and James Russell Lowell 1819-1891, who was Virginia's God Father. There were those her father met at St Ives Arts Club or through his editorship of the Dictionary of National Biography.

Moving in

Leslie Stephen, a sophisticated man of letters, of some wealth and literary renown in the metropolis of London, brought his young family to live in this very different, rather primitive environment of St Ives. The Stephen family were Leslie, with Laura aged 12, from his first marriage to Minny

Thackeray. His wife Julia, with the children from her first marriage to George Duckworth: George 14, Stella 13 and Gerald 12. Leslie was 16 years older than Julia, and at the age of 34 she began another young family of four, with very little respite between the births of Vanessa, Thoby, Virginia and Adrian.

It is in their summer residence, Talland House, that the sisters, Virginia and Vanessa Stephen began their tentative and inspiring journeys into learning their crafts of writing and painting. Virginia Woolf would become the famous writer, and Vanessa would become the noted artist Vanessa Bell.

St Ives Harbour
by Herbert Ivan Babbage 1912

Virginia Woolf & Vanessa Bell – A CHILDHOOD IN ST IVES

Adrian and Virginia

Virginia and Vanessa

Childhood Years

The childhood years in St Ives are captured in the photographs of Vanessa, Thoby, Virginia and Adrian at play in the two to three acres of Talland House garden. The children were unrestricted by the rules of good behaviour expected of them in their London town house. In Cornwall they could run wild down Primrose Valley to Porthminster beach and leave behind their hats and gloves and all the good manners expected of young ladies and gentlemen of society. It was in this small fishing town that Virginia gained an insight into her own sensual being.

Years later, as an adult, we hear the excitement in Virginia as she anticipates travelling by train to the West Country: *Here we are on the verge of going to Cornwall. This time tomorrow – we shall be stepping onto the platform at Penzance, sniffing the air, looking for our trap, and then – Good God! Driving off across the moors to Zennor – Why am I so incredibly and incurably romantic about Cornwall ?* [3]

Lesley b.1832, Julia b.1846, Stella b.1869, Adrian b.1883, Thoby b.1880, Vanessa b.1879, Virginia b.1882. Talland House.

Virginia and Leonard may have been staying with Katherine and Arnold Forster at Eagle's Nest in Zennor, therefore, arriving in Penzance and driving in the trap across the moors would be the quickest way to Zennor. Although Virginia loved the landscape of this area, she considered Eagle's Nest, built on a hill and exposed to the Atlantic, to be a very cold, windy house.

Arrival by train to St Ives

The family arrived by train on the long journey from London's Paddington Station. They changed to the branch line at St Erth, opened in 1877, to enjoy a fifteen minute coastal ride past the bird sanctuary by Lelant village station, to the huge Porthkidney beach, the golf course, and through a wooded area with glimpses to the sea. Nearing the end of their journey they would round a bend and catch their first glimpse of the harbour, at that time still full of the boats of the fishing fleet and alight from the train refreshed by the sight of Porthminster beach, their local playground, spread out before them.

St Ives Station and Porthminster beach with seine boats, 1890s

The small town was easily accessible and the sisters would walk down The Terrace through to the High Street, where at Lanhams shop they would buy their supplies; Virginia her pencils and writing pads and Vanessa her paints and brushes. It was a shop which supplied a great many necessities to the town and provided an art gallery where artists displayed their paintings. This was the first art gallery in town, established in 1887. Close by, in Market Place, the family walked past the 15th century inn, the George and Dragon, demolished in 1887.

They would have been familiar with Curnows, the bakers in the High Street, who had the largest restaurant in town. They did the catering for many functions and, in an interview with the author in the late 1980s, Treve Curnow said: "Father was a master baker and confectioner. We used to do the catering for the Arts Club. On President's night we provided a running buffet. The things we made were out of this world, game pies, fish pies, vol-au-vent, various sandwiches and salads, meringues, iced puddings, French and Genoese pastries, Venetian jellies and creams. They really went to town. The cost was one guinea per head." [4]

Lanhams

Golden Lion (left). George & Dragon 15th century (middle) demolished 1887

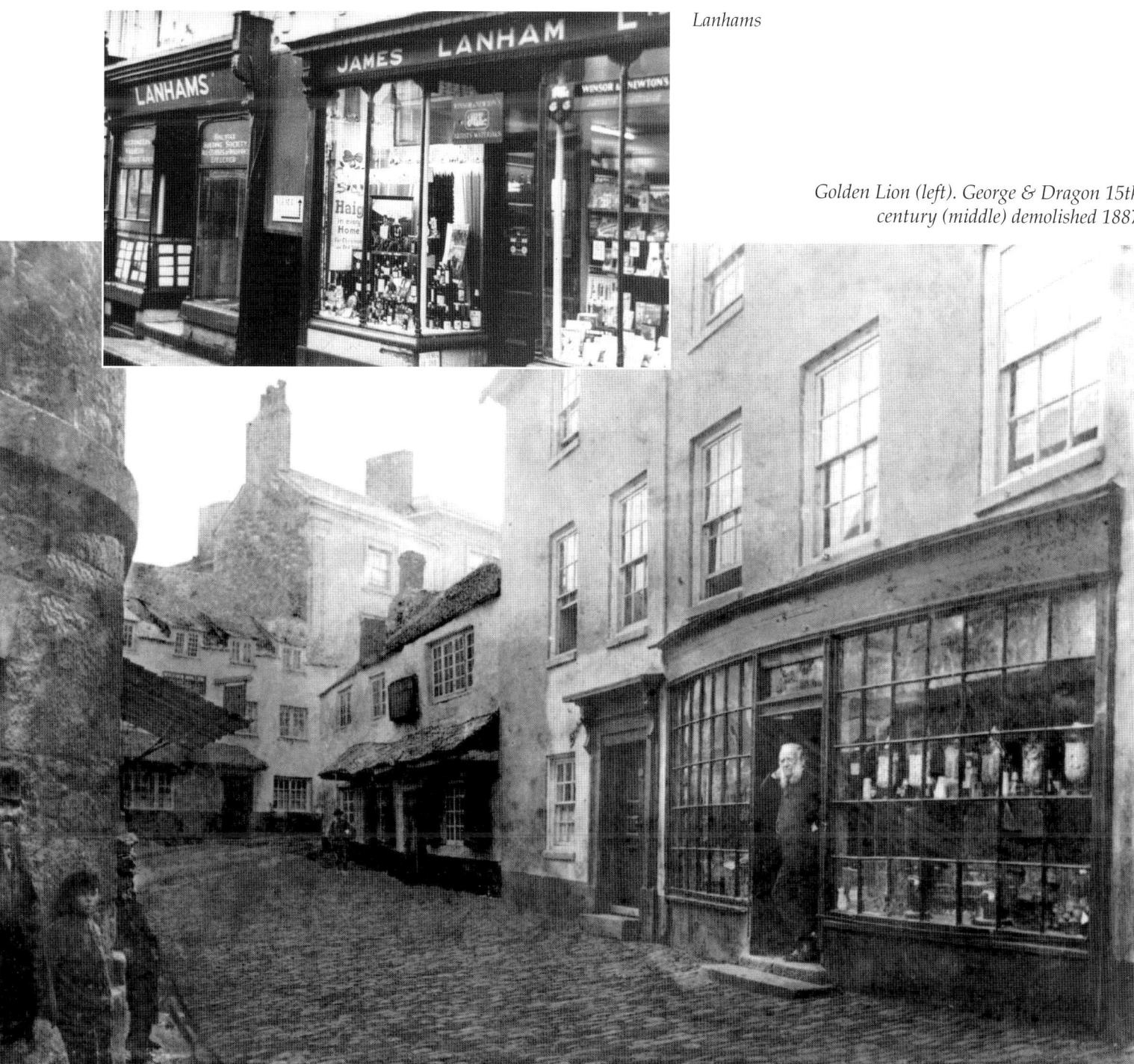

Julia and Leslie

While the children were enjoying their leisure, their parents, Julia and Leslie were engaging themselves with the town and its people. Julia was visiting the sick and underprivileged and providing comfort and support in cases of illness and alleviating want, when nothing was in the larder or purse to sustain the family. This was often to the neglect of her own family, especially of the needy Virginia, but Victorian ladies of wealth were expected to help those less materially fortunate than themselves; Julia needed to embrace this tradition and do her duty. She also encouraged her eldest daughter, Stella, from her first marriage to be like-minded.

Leslie would rather observe the lives of the fishermen than groan with boredom at talk round the dinner table in London. He was a familiar figure on the harbour and had great respect for the fishermen and cared about the hardship and danger to their lives. He had been working as editor of the *Cornhill Magazine* from 1871-1882 and was feeling the release from that responsibility. In that first year in St Ives he wrote to George Smith, with whom he was now engaged as editor of the Dictionary of National Biography. *We are having lovely weather here, and the place is perfectly charming. I think that we have made a great hit in taking the house, which is perfect for our requirements. I shall, I hope, come back ready to write and edit biographies by the dozen.*[5] Many of those biographies were written in St Ives.

Above: *Leslie and Julia Stephen*

Right: *The Harbour, St Ives*

Opposite page: *The Wharf, St Ives*

A Walk in West Penwith

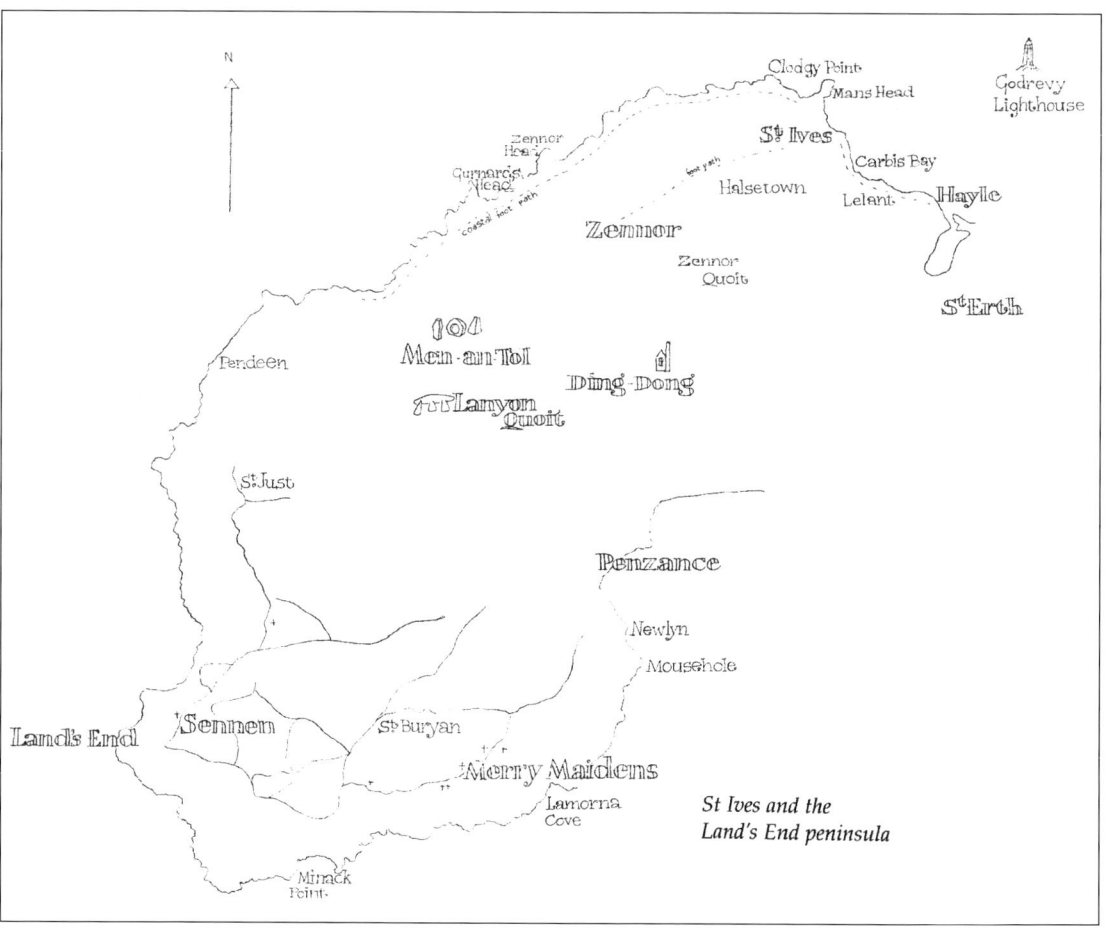

St Ives and the Land's End peninsula

Virginia accompanied her father on various country walks but more reluctantly by Vanessa who, like Lily Briscoe in *To the Lighthouse* preferred to sit and sketch in the garden looking out to Godrevy lighthouse, the sea and Hayle Towans; the sand dunes behind the three miles of beach.

In 1883 Leslie and his nephew Jem [James Kenneth Stephen] were staying at Talland House without the family. In writing to Julia, Leslie described their walk through Halsetown, Towednack, Ding Dong mine and thereby to Land's End. 'We had a glorious day .. the sea was grand ..magnificent breakers right over the rocks.' After lunch they walked back, taking in the circle of nine ancient stones, known as the Merry Maidens, across country to Penzance and the train ride home to St Ives. Leslie assured Julia that although he was 51, she need not worry about his health; he had walked 30 miles that day.

Top left: *Chûn Quoit*

Top right: *Men-an-Tol*

The next day the pair set out for Gurnard's Head: *There we climbed to the top & sat down & had our sandwiches & finished our brandy flask & then I showed him the way down the chimney. I went first .. his right leg jammed between two rocks .. the thickest part of him jammed tight also. I had to come at last & try to pick him out like a periwinkle with a pin* [6] This must be the area's rock climb that Leslie first climbed and recorded for the *Alpine Club* in 1858, when he was only twenty-six: *a rock climb gangling and prehensile.* He was editor of the *Alpine Journal* in 1868, a post he held for four years.

However, in spite of the excitement of his climbing and walking adventures and initiating his nephew Jem into rock climbing, he wrote to Julia, *Tomorrow I shall be home and St Ives a dream. It seems rather like a dream now; for the absence of you & the little ones made it ghostly.*[7] Leslie Stephen was among the first rank of Victorian Golden Age mountaineers and the first climber to record the sport of sea-cliff climbing in Cornwall until surpassed by Arthur Westlake, nephew of the Westlake's of Eagles Nest in Zennor and friends of the Stephens.

Right: *Leslie Stephen*

Far right: *Cliffs and Sea Pinks*

Leslie's Sunday tramps often included the children if there were no adults to match him stride for stride across the wild moors. Ten year old Virginia, writing in her personal newspaper The Hyde Park Gate News and experimenting with journalism, observed that Mr Stephen, *who is a renowned pedestrian, walked to St Erth in preference to going by locomotive*. She also wrote: *Mr Stephen with his daughter Miss Vanessa Stephen and his son Mr Thoby Stephen went for a walk to Penzance. The real object of the walk was to visit an old British village* [Chysauster] *which is situated about four miles from Penzance and which takes the walker a little out of his way to visit .. it is a most venerable and interesting edifice.*[8]

VIRGINIA WOOLF

Sea Cliffs at Land's End
by Borlase Smart

Below left: *Cape Cornwall*

Below right: *St Michael's Mount*

45

The Ragamice

The Ragamice was Leslie's pet name for his youngest children, Vanessa, Thoby, Virginia, and Adrian. Twelve year old Laura, his only child from his first marriage, was proving difficult to manage. She had been born prematurely and was slow to develop; her behaviour was unpredictable, with frequent bouts of bad temper and she chatted incessantly. In those days she was classed as an idiot. She was eventually put into a home for the mentally deficient and although in the early years she was visited, mostly by Stella and her father, she died in an institution at the age of 75. But in the early days Leslie and Julia had hopes for her. While in St Ives negotiating the lease for Talland House, he wrote to Julia and slipped in a note for Laura: *My darling Laura, I am in a beautiful place called St Ives. We shall come in the summer I hope. There is a beautiful beach for the little ones. You will bathe there and learn to swim. . . . It is a very nice house, with a garden and a fountain and grapes and strawberries and peaches. I hope that you have been good. It makes me very unhappy if mother tells me you have been naughty. Your loving father.* [9]

Porthminster Beach with bathing huts.

Porthminster Beach
by Sydney Mortimer Laurence

While the children played on the beach, Julia and Leslie would have their special place on the rocks looking out to sea, at their own local Porthminster beach. In these first couple of years at Talland House, Leslie would often come to St Ives on his own to supervise various improvements that Old Lobb, the gardener and caretaker, would be carrying out. Heather and gorse were planted by the tennis ground, a pond was being dug; a garden seat for Julia was in place and roses planted to provide a bower. He reported to Julia that the grapes were growing well in their glasshouses, and there would be plenty of potatoes to harvest.

However, he missed his wife and having the children, the 'ragamice', around him. One summer visitor to Talland House in 1882, the sister of Walter Sickert, wrote that she, 'had the most romantic holiday of my life' with the Stephen family, and described Leslie: *We had seen his gaunt figure with the ragged red brown beard, striding over the moors, a dog at his heels. He was a formidable man, with an immensely high forehead, steely-blue eyes and a long pointed nose. We watched with delight his naked babies running about the beach or being towed into the sea between his legs.* [10]

Talland House with gardens and greenhouses

But Virginia held a special place in her father's heart. It was she who raided his library for books and, along with her mother, satisfied his need for admiration and affection. Virginia could charm her father and play the coquette with impunity. In writing to Julia in 1893, when Virginia was eleven, Leslie reported the daily happenings: *Little Ginia is already an accomplished flirt. I said today that I must go down to my work. She nestled herself down on the sofa by me; squeezed her little self tightly up against me and then gazed up with her bright eyes through her shock of hair and said, "Don't go, Papa!" She looked full of mischief all the time. I never saw such a little rogue.*[11].

Julia and Leslie involved themselves in the children's education at home, and also with their games. Julia entertained them with writing her amusing stories and reading to them, and Leslie in taking them into the countryside: *Yesterday we went to Trencrom. The children had their inevitable nets, for they are quite mad about bugs.*[12] And Stella noted in her diary: *Father & the three* [Thoby, Virginia and Adrian] *sailed after lunch with old Roach. Mother, Nessa & I went to Hain*[s].[13] [Treloyhan Manor.]

Sophia Farrell began working for the Stephens in 1886, finally retiring in 1931

St Ives Servants

Many of the servants who catered for Talland House lived in cottages in Primrose Valley, which the children passed on their way to Porthminster beach. Alice Curnow laundered for the family. Mrs Adams brought their fish, and lobsters, which were alive in the basket and there were the daily deliveries of bread, meat and household groceries, all pushed by young men with their hand carts up the drive to Sophie's kitchen.

Sophie Farrell, their cook, was part of the household in St Ives and their London house. She maintained a lifelong attachment to the Stephen family which spanned fifty years. She remembered their childhood games and adventures in St Ives. Virginia writes with affection: *Sophie's kitchen was directly beneath our night nursery. We would let down a basket on a string and dangle it over the kitchen window, at night while dinner was going on. If she were in a good temper, the basket would be drawn in and laden with something left from the grown-ups dinner; but if she were in a bad temper, the basket would be jerked in and the string cut.*[14] One wonders if the cook was taken on at St Ives because Farrell is a St Ives name.

Talland House far right of Porthminster Hotel 1894

Artists and Writers

Leslie Stephen wrote to his writer and intellectual friend, Charles Eliot Norton 1827-1908, in America that St Ives attracted him more than ever: *We have even made a pleasant acquaintance with some of the school of artists wh. has strangely sprung up here within the last three or four years. We have even a little picture gallery! One of them is a Yankee named Simmons who once attended your lectures & is married to a lovely Californian. Another is one Adrian Stokes, who sells pictures now for good prices & has an Austrian wife.* [15]

Edward E. Simmons's wife Vesta, and Marianne Stokes, were painters in their own right. From their earliest age Virginia and Vanessa were exposed to a world of writers and artists. Vanessa would have seen the work of artists hanging in James Lanham's gallery, established in 1887, and met them while buying her paints in Lanham's art shop. And of course, Talland House was the meeting place for many artists and writers.

That Leslie Stephen was aware of developments in the artists' community is evidence that the Stephen family were indeed familiar with the artists and the Arts Club activities. In 1892 we have

Left to right:
Marianne Stokes 1890
Adrian Stokes 1890
Edward E Simmons 1890

Moonlight *by Adrian Stokes*

Virginia reporting that, *The St Ives Mrs Simmons came to luncheon. She gave Miss Vanessa Stephen a tie which was not duly appreciated.* [16]   The gift was a present for Vanessa's birthday. The Simmons lived at 23 The Terrace. Another member of the Arts Club was Bosch-Reitz whose portrait of Leslie was hung in the Royal Academy Summer Exhibition of 1890. The *Spectator* reported: *There is one other capital portrait in the Gallery . . it is a head of Mr Leslie Stephen. It is pleasant to record this association of Art and Literature in the persons of Mr Bosch-Reitz, the popular St Ives artist, and his subject, Mr Leslie Stephen, who from long residence may almost be claimed a St Ives man.* [17]

Note: No trace of this portrait has been found.

A St Ives Man

Leslie and Julia Stephen and family were part of the town of St Ives and they took an interest in events, whether it was socialising with friends, or mixing with the local inhabitants and involving themselves in the general welfare of the town. Swimming was a great sport in St Ives and every year on Regatta Day championship races of boating and swimming took place in the harbour. There was a carnival atmosphere, and decorations and flags and brass bands celebrated the day. The four Stephen children watched the display: *we went onto the Malakoff and stood in the crowd and listened to the blare of music wafted across the water; and then a gun was fired and off went the boats, racing round the bay; or the swimmers plunged. And we could see the little heads bobbing in the water and the arms flashing.* [18]   In 1892 Leslie was vice president of the St Ives Swimming and Sailing Association.

Certainly the Stephens were more involved in local affairs than is generally known. In the General Election of 1892 Mr Bedford Bolitho, MP visited St Ives to address a meeting at the Public Hall. It was presided over by Leslie Stephen, who said he was very glad to have a share with his fellow townsmen in discharging an important political duty. Mrs Julia Stephen and Miss Stella Duckworth were noted in the audience. Mr and Mrs Bolitho were among the visitors at Talland House. The Bolitho family had a bank in St Ives.

Are you Ready
by W H Bartlett c 1900

Visitors

Leslie attracted many prominent members of the literary world who desired to visit him in St Ives. In 1884 the American novelist Henry James was lodging at the Tregenna Castle Hotel. He visited again in 1886. The critic Edmund Gosse and his wife Nellie were staying at the same hotel in 1890. He wrote: *We went to St Ives to be near Leslie Stephen, with whom I took immense walks of a wholly speechless character. He and I went to the wrestling at Redruth I remember.* [19]   Stella recorded another event in her diary: *Father & Georgie went off by 11 o'clock train to Truro to see wrestling .The wrestlers returned at 7 having had a good time.* [20]

Tregenna Castle

The writer George Meredith, writer, friend and fellow Sunday Tramp, was several times a guest at Talland House or staying at Tregenna Castle and at 8 Belmont Terrace. Others invited to Talland House were the artists Edward Burne Jones, John Everett Milais, George Frederick Watts and many others. In 1892 Mrs Holman Hunt, wife of William Holman Hunt, Pre-Raphaelite artist, was staying with a party at 5 The Terrace. Virginia wrote in her Hyde Park Gate News for August:

Mrs Hunt and her daughter and son arrived at the terminus of St Ives on Wednesday. Mrs and Miss Vanessa Stephen went down to see them arrive. They came the train not being even half an hour late. They went up quickly to their lodgins [sic] which had been engaged for them by Mrs Stephen. [21]

Other Writers

The novelist Compton Mackenzie, who wrote plays for the Arts Club and whose sister Fay, the actress, performed in them, was introduced to the Club by the writer Charles Marriott. Mackenzie, in his autobiography *My Life and Times* recalled Leslie Stephen entertaining a large gathering at Talland House. He would act as editor for writers who gave their manuscripts to him to read before submitting them for publication.

Sir Compton Mackenzie's first novel was *The Passionate Elopement* 1911, his second novel, *Carnival* 1912 was filmed in Cornwall and his novel *Whisky Galore* and *Monarch of the Glen*, were filmed and televised in Scotland.

Charles Marriott

In 1908 Marriott was president of St Ives Arts Club and, as such, he wrote an article for the *Daily Mail* on the state of the artists' colony: *At the present moment, of the eighty odd studios in this little town of St Ives there is not a single one to let. Cornwall is becoming more and more emphatically the centre of English art, and this winter marks the highest point the development has yet reached.* [21a]

Charles Marriott spent seven years at 3 Porthminster Terrace, with his wife and two daughters. It was there his son was born and where he wrote his first successful novel *The House on the Sands* published in 1909. Marriott moved to London to become art critic for *The Times* and so became acquainted with the work of the Bloomsbury painters.

Marriott invited Hugh Walpole to stay at their house in St Ives, where he encouraged his first attempt at a novel *The Wooden Horse*. It was published in 1909 and was praised by E M Forster. Later, Hugh Walpole and Virginia Woolf exchanged opinions on various writers of the day.

Godrevy Island and Lighthouse

Godrevy Lighthouse

Across the bay from Talland House was the iconic Godrevy Lighthouse standing on its natural island and shining its beamed light into the bedrooms bringing comfort and reassurance to children who couldn't sleep. It was the inspiration for Virginia's novel *To the Lighthouse*.

When the St Ives Arts Club was established in 1890, in a building at Westcotts Quay on the edge of the sea, Leslie and Julia Stephen were invited to join, and although there is no documentary evidence, to support it, the children at Talland House might have attended many concerts, plays and parties enjoyed at the Club. They may also have stood at its window, overlooking the harbour and out to Godrevy Lighthouse, whose light Vanessa and Virginia *saw night by night shine across the bay into the windows of Talland House.* [21b] Indeed, whether by night or day, Godrevy lighthouse, standing sentinel on its lonely island just off shore at Gwithian, seemed to be their constant companion. A local boy, Donald Bray, writes of his memories of its beam:

I used to lie in bed watching the beams of Godrevy lighthouse revolving. Their rays would sweep across the ceiling of my bedroom overlooking the Bay. I do remember it as a real comfort, with Trevose Head lighthouse away on the horizon.[22]

Godrevy Lighthouse 1900s

Godrevy lighthouse was built in 1859. Its light was described as a bold flashing white beam, and was manned by two keepers. Since 1934 the beam has operated automatically, its light no more than a faint glimmer at ten second intervals, and the small island is now deserted but for the gulls.

The light had a range of 12 miles. Extending from the island on which the lighthouse perches is a mile-and-a-half length of reef known as The Stones. These are marked by a black pillar-type buoy with whistle and bell, warning of this dangerous reef, responsible for many shipwrecks. One of the earliest wrecks was in1649, when the *Garland*, bound for France, dragged her anchor while sheltering in St Ives Bay. She was carrying the possessions of the recently executed Charles the First. It is rumoured that gold buttons have been washed ashore on the three miles beach at Hayle.

Above: *The Dow Family at Talland House 1912*

Left: *The Stephen Family at Talland House 1890s*

Return to St Ives

In 1895 tragedy struck a terrible blow to the Stephen family with the death of their mother. Their father could not countenance a life in St Ives without Julia and never returned to Talland House again. However, in 1905, after the death of their father, the four Stephen children travelled back to St Ives to relive those joyful childhood days. Leslie had sold the lease to the artist, Thomas Millie Dow and his wife Florence and their children, who were happily living and enjoying the rooms and gardens of Talland House as the Stephen family had done.

They visited the house and peered through the escallonia hedge and were surprised at its still familiar appearance. It was as though they had left it yesterday. The Dows invited the Stephen family to tea and Virginia found them delightful. The Dows had their own Jersey cow, chickens, ducks, a horse, a two-wheeled Italian trap and a dog cart for travelling around. They had enlarged the house and an artist's studio was built for Thomas in the field across Talland Road.

In later years Elsie, Florence Millie Dow's eldest daughter from her first marriage, was grandmother to four granddaughters who lived at Talland House. Alison, one of the girls remembered

Florence Millie Dow, nee Pilcher 1908
Thomas Millie Dow 1908
Paintings by William Strang

the house and had fond memories of her childhood. She wrote in a personal memoir. 'All the rooms were papered in delicate faded patterns of a greeny grey colour of William Morris design. All the woodwork was white painted. The floors, apart from the kitchen and nursery quarters which were cork matting and lino, were polished wood covered with large worn Turkish rugs.'

Alison describes the house with its many rooms and its views across the bay, and the capacious gardens with an abundance of roses and grapes from the greenhouse and vegetables and prize winning flowers grown by the gardener; of the crochet lawn, the cricket pitch and wild areas, which were ideal for 'games, garden teas or just idling and the stream tumbled down splashing into a pool where we rinsed the sand out of our bathing suits.' The young Alison and her sisters climbed a small stairway to the flat roof which was surrounded by a white painted balustrade, from which they enjoyed a panoramic view of sea and coastline. It was an especially good spot to view fireworks on bonfire night, as the young Stephen children experienced. They were especially fond of firework parties. Virginia wrote in her Hyde Park Gate News when she was 10, that her brother Thoby had celebrated his twelfth birthday in St Ives and there was 'a splendid display of fireworks.'

As an adult, Alison Symons thought of Virginia Woolf's childhood at Talland House, an experience very like her own, with her love of the house and garden and understood how such influences formed the nucleus for the novel *To the Lighthouse*.

Virginia and Vanessa as Companions

The two Stephen girls cared for each other from an early age, with Vanessa, the eldest by three years, capable and reliable, concerned for the frailer, more complex, Virginia. *It thus came about that Nessa and I formed together a very close conspiracy… we formed our private nucleus.* [23]

They were good and constant companions and often worked together, one painting or drawing, the other either reading to herself, or reading aloud. They walked together to Kensington Gardens and skated on the Round Pond when it was frozen over, where ' a chatty old gentleman talked to Nessa of St Ives and cricket'. Virginia recorded meticulously in *A Passionate Apprentice* Vanessa's attendance at her painting lessons: *Nessa went to her studio* begins a diary entry for every Monday, Wednesday and Friday. *Nessa had to walk down to the studio because of the wind*. She was usually to be seen flying off on her bike. *She brought me back North and South*, [Mrs Gaskell] *which I shall read out aloud to Nessa*. She also read Dickens's *David Copperfield*. *Nessa went to have her* [lunch] *at an ABC near the studio, so as to get in as much drawing as possible. . . I walked to Kensington Square and then to the studio, to fetch Nessa back*.[24]

Virginia wrote of how often they were together in their activities. In Brighton: 'Nessa and I sat on the beach – Nessa attempting a picture of the Pier, & I reading Barchester Towers [Anthony Trollope] to myself.' In Gloucester: In the afternoon we went for a walk to an old house which Nessa painted, a house with lions on the gate posts & a sun dial.' At Painswick: 'She is painting from the summer house, and Nessa painted a little down at the bottom of the garden. Nessa painting and I reading.'

The visual arts in all its forms were of interest to Vanessa. In 1897 a new camera was bought and tested out on holiday. Stella and her brothers were well versed in taking photographs. In 1892 Virginia writes in her Hyde Park Gate News that, *She* [Miss Stillman] *was photographed incessantly by Miss Stella Duckworth and Mr Gerald Duckworth who keep a visitor's list by photographing everyone who comes to the palatial residence.*[25]

Virginia was referring to Talland House. Their great aunt, Julia Margaret Cameron, was a professional portraitist, but Vanessa's camera records informally the family, and visits of friends, as compiled by Quentin Bell and Angelica Garnett in the book *Vanessa Bell's Family Album*. Virginia writes of their adventures with the camera at Bognor :

We tried shutting Nessa up in the cupboard to put in the films, but there were too many chinks. Then she suggested being covered by her quilt, and everything else that I could lay hands on and she was accordingly, buried in dresses and dressing gowns till no light could penetrate. Soon she emerged almost stifled having forgotten how to put the film in. [26]

This was eventually achieved and she took photos of Stella and Jack on the sands. Back home at Hyde Park Gate, in the night nursery, Nessa and Ginnie developed ten successful photos.

Brother George

As Virginia and Vanessa grew up their step brother George attempted to introduce his beautiful sisters into society, to attend parties and balls, to enjoy the theatre, to meet eligible young men, to accept invitations to dine and to mix in elegant social circles. Virginia and Vanessa were bored by such pretentious people and neither of them could be persuaded to tolerate the inane and unintelligent, or to dress for special occasions. George complained of Vanessa's dumb silence and of Virginia's voluble discourses at his carefully arranged meetings with the right kind of people. They were invariably persons of rank and nobility – quite unlike the cultural and intellectual society found by Virginia and Vanessa in Bloomsbury, where they had recently moved, after the death of their father in 1904.

Gordon Square, with its chintzes and plain washed walls offered freedom and a different lifestyle, the family was staying up late, entertaining friends, drinking coffee after dinner instead of tea, going to concerts and visiting picture galleries. Virginia remembered that at the Grafton gallery they were lectured on Impressionism.

While Vanessa may have been overawed by some of her art teachers, Virginia entertained no importance to their paintings, expertise, status in the art world, and their self-aggrandizement. She exercised a critical and sardonic eye on the professors and their followers.

In 1903 Vanessa and Virginia were invited to 'an artistic party,' the Royal Academy's annual reception at Burlington House. Virginia commented wryly:

We drifted about, gazing at human pictures mostly, with snatches of desultory talk. We looked with admiration at those ladies, who are the high aristocrats of such gatherings as these – who know the President & all the more distinguished academicians. Their demeanour is beautiful . . I am always impressed by the splendid superiority of these artist men and women over their Philistine brethren.[27]

In 1905 Virginia noted in her diary: *Snow to sit to Nessa*. Margery Snowden was a student friend of Vanessa's. Shortly afterwards, she was engaged on a painting of Lady Robert Cecil. The following month we hear of the progress of the portrait. *Nessa painting Nelly, who sits now in her own drawing room, by the window, with a green curtain & Troper* [her dog] *at her feet.*[27a]

Vanessa exhibited a work at the New English Art Club, her first show, with a portrait of Lady Robert Cecil. Virginia wrote:

April 1905. A morning devoted to art! – happily successful. I went off after breakfast to the New Gallery which might or might not have hung the Nelly picture – & to my great relief found it in the Catalogue, & saw it hang fairly in the gallery, which is quite a cheerful beginning. Dashed home & general rejoicing of a mild description. Went in the afternoon with Adrian & Nessa (most unwillingly) to the show again.[28]

Virginia and Vanessa Study at Home

While Thoby and Adrian gained an education at Cambridge University, their parents did not see fit to educate their two brilliant daughters. Virginia taught herself languages. She received some coaching in Latin and Greek but she was self-motivated and studied history and read biographies of the important people of the day, as well as learning about the ancient myths and civilisations of the past. At an early age the girls were taught by Julia and Leslie and various home tutors. Julia was the hub around which everything turned and on whom everyone relied and Virginia always remembered her in a room filled with people. Hyde Park Gate and Talland House were full of her vital presence but Virginia barely had her mother to herself.

Virginia and Vanessa, very much commanded their own schooling. Vanessa had the confidence to enrol herself in the Royal Academy and Slade School of Art and progress to be one of the early innovators of Modernism and a member of the Bloomsbury group of painters. Virginia, it seems, had no need of outside direction or training, only writing, writing and more writing and enduring the criticism of friends and other authors on the completion of a book and feeling drained of energy once her characters were self-sufficient and she was free of their demands. However, it was maddening to know that their parents spent thousands on Thoby and Adrian's education, and barely hundreds on the two girls.

St Ives again

Following their first successful return visit to St Ives, three years later in 1908, Virginia wrote to Lytton Strachey from the sitting room of her lodgings at Trevose House, Draycott Terrace, where she had a good view of the town and harbour and where, having cleared away several small domestic items, she sat at the dining room table to write. Virginia recorded in her diary that she wrote all morning and Vanessa painted all afternoon.

Mrs Proudfoot, a St Ives woman who was a child at the time, said that many artists stayed at Trevose, her mother's house. Julius Olsson, a fine seascape painter, visited often and Gertrude Talmage, artist and tutor, would live with them for six months at a time. She remembers the occasion when Virginia arrived: "In 1908 Miss Stephen lodged with my mother. She came to St Ives on her own. She went walking on the moors. She was a bit of an eccentric." [29] She remembered nothing of the arrival of Vanessa.

However, Virginia was shortly followed by Vanessa and Clive Bell, who had married in 1907 and a year later Vanessa had baby Julian. The family had travelled the long journey on the Great Western Railway from Paddington to alight at St Ives station. Vanessa had forwarded instructions to Virginia:

Don't give up the best bedroom, for you will want it to sit in probably and Clive and I shall want separate rooms. He tried here sleeping in the dressing room, but gave it up as he couldn't get to sleep again after once

Virginia Woolf & Vanessa Bell - A CHILDHOOD IN ST IVES

View from Draycott Terrace showing the Harbour and Porthminster beach 2014

being waked by Julian. We shall get to St Ives at 7.10 Friday. Will you order a short vehicle to bring me and the nurse and baby from the station with one box and perambulator, and unless they should arrive beforehand also another two boxes, Julian's cradle and bath.[30]

Virginia returned from this holiday before the Bells and Vanessa wrote to her sister that they had come struggling back from the beach, all uphill, up Primrose Valley, where she had been sketching the sea, and Virginia's dog had interrupted the games of a family of children.

It was at this time that a flirtation took place between Virginia and Clive, both pushed to the background by Vanessa's preoccupation with the infant Julian. They were apparently consoling each other for Vanessa's neglect of them. It is an indication of the pivotal role that Vanessa played in the circle of family and friends that surrounded her.

There was also a Trevose House at Carbis Bay where the family stayed. The houses were named after Trevose lighthouse, which lies further north-east on the Cornish coast. Virginia wrote from Carbis Bay that they worked every day and that her sister had achieved some of her best work. *Nessa produces two canvases a day; and is mad with the difficulties of the sea.*[31]

Trevose House

Lelant Hotel

In 1909 we find an impulsive Virginia writing to Vanessa to explain her sudden absence from London:

I went for a walk in Regents Park yesterday morning, and it suddenly struck me how absurd it was to stay in London, with Cornwall going on all the time. I bought an ABC and found there was a train at one o'clock. It was then 12.30. However I caught it, and arrived at 10.30 last night. I have no pocket handkerchief, watch, key, notepaper, spectacles, cheque book, looking glass or coat. However, it is a hot spring day. I have been walking along the sands and sitting in the sun .. I am so drugged with fresh air that I can't write .. As for the beauty of this place, it surpasses every other season. I have the hotel to myself – and get a very nice sitting room for nothing. How I wish you were coming out with me now – it is very warm – bright blue sky and sea, and no wind and smells heavenly.[32]

Virginia was staying at the Lelant Hotel, now the Badger Inn.

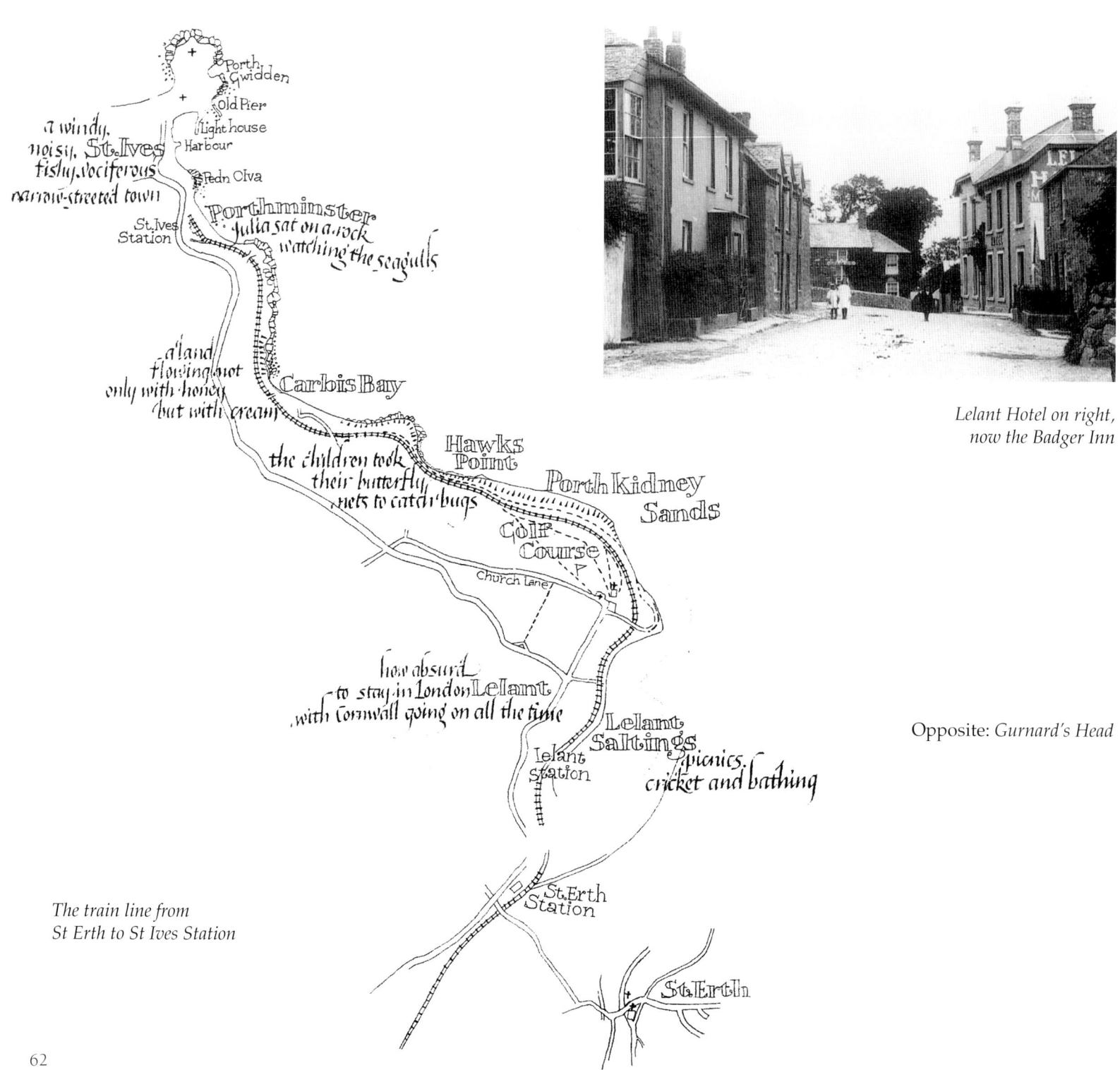

Lelant Hotel on right, now the Badger Inn

Opposite: Gurnard's Head

The train line from St Erth to St Ives Station

A Walking Tour

The following year, 1910, when Vanessa's second son, Quentin, was born, Virginia and Jean Thomas, took a walking tour in Cornwall. Her companion had been Virginia's carer at the nursing home in Twickenham. This was part of a recuperation expedition – Cornwall being the usual place for Virginia's recovery after illness or a panacea to ward off another attack of depression. The women walked extensively in some of Virginia's favourite places, into the moors and usually in sight of the sea, as at Gurnard's Head, where they sat and surveyed the boats and smelled the gorse and noted the wild flowers and Virginia satiated herself in the perfumes of Cornwall. They stayed at the remote and quite primitive Porthmeor Farm belonging to the Berrymans.

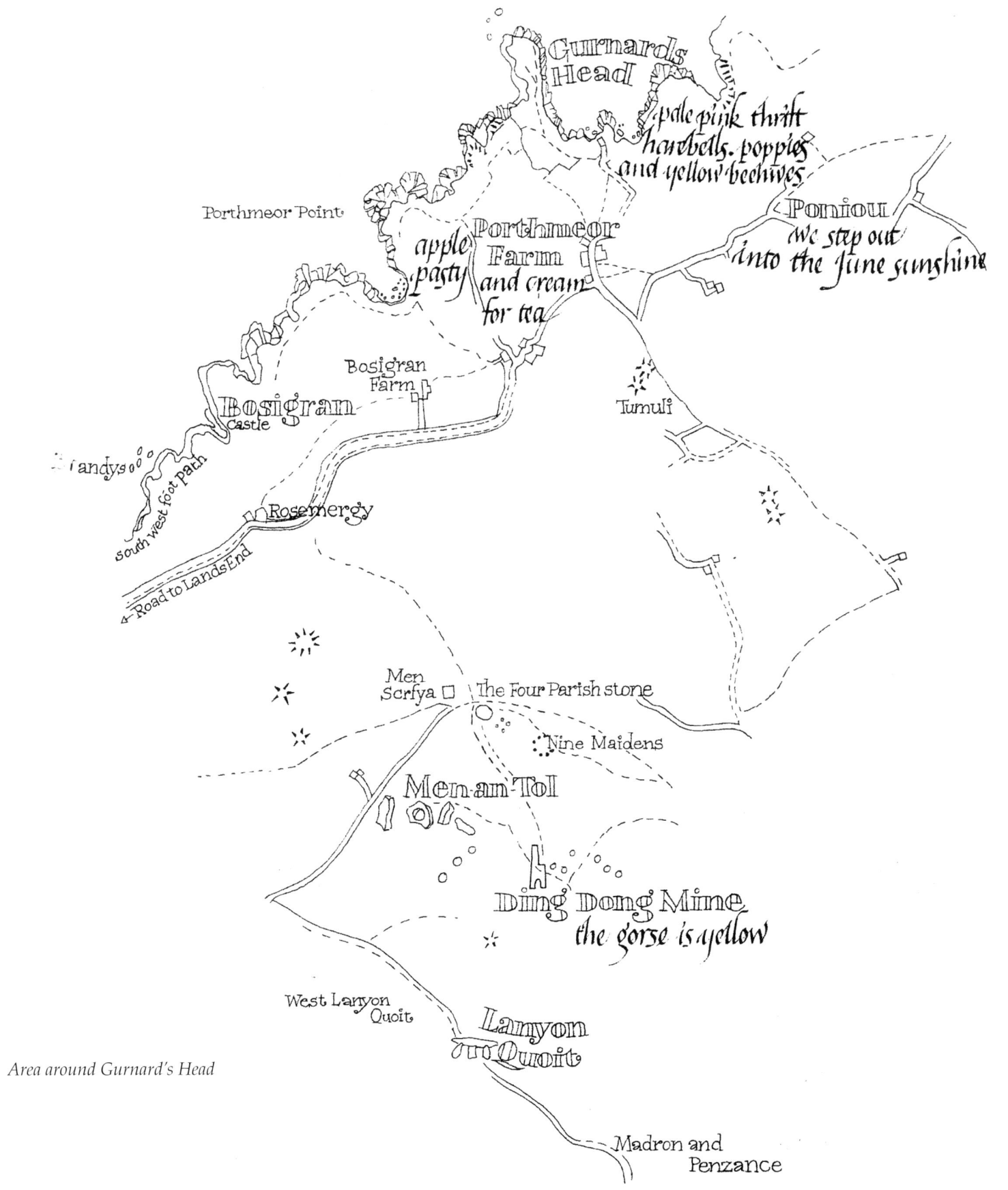

Area around Gurnard's Head

Marrying Leonard

In 1912 Virginia married Leonard Woolf. He gave her the stability she needed throughout her life, in times of dire stress and illness. He was her rock and although he couldn't provide a cure, his support through the worst times of her mental and physical breakdowns was invaluable. Indeed, in her final letter to Leonard, Virginia admits, 'I owe all the happiness of my life to you.' He and Vanessa were constantly faithful during these extreme times. Although everything appeared to be flourishing, one year later Virginia suffered a severe nervous breakdown. For two years after their marriage Virginia was unstable and had attempted suicide.

In St Ives in 1913 Mrs Arnold Forster, a friend of Vanessa and Virginia known in the Bloomsbury circle as Ka Cox, (Katherine) was staying in the town. She visited the St Ives Arts Club as a guest and was signed in by Daisy Whitehouse, one of three artist sisters who were living in St Ives. Katherine Cox was a good friend to Virginia and nursed her during an illness. When she and Arnold Forster bought Eagle's Nest Virginia and Leonard were often visitors to the house.

Portrait of Virginia by Vanessa 1912
© National Portrait Gallery

Porthmeor Farm, where Virginia stayed in 1910

Eagle's Nest *by Borlase Smart*

In 1914 Leonard brought Virginia to Cornwall. Always, it had a restorative effect on Virginia's state of mind. They travelled around to various places one of them the Carbis Bay Hotel, where I discovered their entry for April 1914 written in the visitors' book.

The Memoir Club

There were bright moments in the turmoil of Virginia's experiences of extreme mental confusion and in 1913, the Memoir Club was formed. Virginia and Vanessa met their cerebral equals in an exclusive company of friends. They dined, read memoirs, talked about religion, art and sex – inappropriate in mixed society. They enjoyed meeting some of their brother Thoby's university friends. Virginia soon realized that the majority of these men were not attracted to women. *There were buggers in Trinity College, Cambridge; but it never occurred to me that there were buggers even now in the Stephens' sitting room at Gordon Square.*[33] At first, in the company of these Lords of the universe with their Cambridge University education, Virginia felt rather intimated, but soon learned that she was their equal. The club petered out during the First World War, but in 1920 they reformed, with some new members but with largely the same crew as before, Lytton Strachey, Clive Bell, Duncan Grant, Morgan Forster, Leonard Woolf, John Maynard Keynes, Desmond MacCarthy, David Garnett; and Roger Fry became an important member.

Vanessa, Stella, Virginia as young adults

Virginia the writer

In writing of Virginia Woolf there is plenty of material to draw upon and to quote. She was a prolific letter writer; she kept a journal and a diary. She was a productive essayist, wrote articles, reviews, literary criticism, plays and biographies, lectured and taught. Foremost, she was the essential novelist, the creative writer of modern fiction, for which she gained her place among the contemporary English writers of the 20th century. Her reputation is built upon the 'stream of consciousness' in a modernist style where the words flow immediately from her thoughts to the page. That is not to say there were no revisions, for in rewriting she suffered great distress; she complained about her capacity for feeling with intensity. Her ideas were largely based upon her frame of mind, emotions and response to what she saw, heard and experienced and she remained true to those first thoughts. In her diary she says, *writing is effort; writing is despair.* In another diary entry, volume 1V 1931-1935 she writes, *I finished my re-typing of The Waves. Not that it is finished – oh dear no. For then I must correct the re-re-typing.*

The Hogarth Press

In 1917 Virginia and Leonard Woolf set up their own printing press, producing their first book, *Two Stories,* written by each of them and illustrated by the artist Dora Carrington. Vanessa admired these woodcuts and soon began her own uneasy alliance with the press in illustrating Virginia's novels; refusing to be guided by Leonard in what to design. They later resolved their differences and Vanessa's woodcut illustrations remained untouched by Leonard.

Katherine Mansfield was the first writer invited to publish with The Hogarth Press. Ottoline Morrell had loaned Virginia's first novel, *The Voyage Out*, published by Duckworth in 1915, to Katherine, who had praised it. Virginia was aware of Katherine's writing and felt that she was one of the few people with whom she could discuss her work, indeed, Virginia was setting the press for her story *Prelude* while writing her own novel *Night and Day*. These two writers were always conscious and critical of the other's achievements and yet they were friends, sometimes enemies, and admirers too.

In 1918 Virginia paid regular visits to Katherine in East Heath Street, Hampstead, a grey painted house which Katherine named, The Elephant. Virginia was shocked at the deterioration in her appearance from the ravaging effects of tuberculosis. She was never to recover from this disease and died abroad in 1923.

Working the press was laborious and hard – an extreme learning curve for two amateur printer publishers. Everything from printing, binding, checking, packing and posting was entirely Virginia and Leonard's responsibility until they were up and running. They employed a number of young men and women, who passed through their doors, uninspired by the experience. One such employee was Ralph Partridge, later to marry Dora Carrington. Another was Frances Marshall, who became the second wife of Ralph Partridge. Frances outlived most of the Bloomsbury group and wrote about them in her book *Memories* in 1981. Frances worked for one day at the Hogarth Press but left the same day, unable to come to terms with 'that press.'

The Hogarth Press brought Virginia and Leonard into contact with many writers and new found friends. Katherine Mansfield and Virginia were frequent visitors to Garsington Manor, Ottoline Morrell's famous house and garden, where Ottoline cultivated the writers and artists of the day, often offering financial support and encouragement for their endeavours. One such beneficiary was D H Lawrence who, unkindly, made Ottoline a figure of fun in his novel *Women in Love* written in Cornwall.

In 1922 Vanessa designed a woodcut book jacket for Hogarth Press. It was Virginia's novel *Jacob's Room*, the first of three books where St Ives was at the heart of the story. The other two were *The Waves* and *To the Lighthouse*; the latter by which she is best known. That same year Vanessa's woodcut fronted Virginia's novel *Kew Gardens*. Their collaborative work continued over Virginia's writing life, with Vanessa producing the distinctive cover designs for all the books.

The book that most illustrated the collaboration and emotional input of Vanessa and Virginia was the novel *To the Lighthouse* 1927 in which Virginia recreated their parents and their childhood at Talland House. Vanessa confirmed the accuracy of the portrait of their mother, and how moved she was by Virginia's written portrayal of both parents. It was probably the one time when Vanessa felt words conveyed personality, nature and character better than a painted picture: *so you see as far as portrait painting goes, you seem to me to be a supreme artist. I think it is your best work* [34] Of the fictional painter in the novel, Vanessa wrote: *By the way, surely Lily Briscoe must have been rather a good painter – before her time perhaps, but with great gifts really?*.[35] Does this question mark say 'are you talking about me Virginia?

In describing Mr Ramsay, alias Leslie Stephen, Virginia is harsh about his tyrannical behaviour: *He is petty, selfish, vain, egotistical; he is spoilt; he is a tyrant; he wears Mrs Ramsay to death;* Here Virginia reveals her anger with her father, knowing how he relied on their mother and demanded her admiration and attention to an excess, which tired her, but Leonard Woolf felt both Virginia and Vanessa were at times overly critical of their father, a judgement based on knowing all the family: *Having known Leslie Stephen in the flesh and having heard an enormous deal about him from his children, I feel pretty sure that .. Mr Ramsey* [sic] *is a pretty good fictional portrait of Leslie Stephen – and yet there are traces of unfairness to Stephen in Ramsey. Leslie Stephen must have been in many ways an exasperating man within the family and he exasperated his daughters, particularly Vanessa.*[36]

Virginia was thirteen when her mother died in 1895. Years had to pass before she could confront the past. She had written *To the Lighthouse* very quickly, and afterwards she was no longer obsessed by her mother; of being stirred by emotions, of hearing her voice, thinking of her gestures, or writing at her desk, or sitting in the garden watching her children play cricket. Virginia remembered her mother coming into her bedroom at Talland House to see if she was asleep and recalled how she longed for her to come with her lighted candle.

Vanessa was also busy consulting with Virginia about designs and colours in Monk's House which Virginia and Leonard bought in 1919. Of particular importance is the tiled fireplace in Virginia's bedroom, which Vanessa designed and made as a birthday present and to celebrate her sister's

novel *To the Lighthouse*. The central theme is the view from Talland House; there is the bay, with a Cornish lugger and Godrevy Lighthouse.

E M Forster's opinion of *The Waves,* 1931, the third in the St Ives trilogy, drew from him the comment that his excitement over it came from believing that 'one's encountered a classic'. He promises to write again when he has reread it. His own book *A Room with a View* was published this same year. The letter from Morgan Forster gave Virginia more pleasure than any comments she had received from any other book. Virginia and Vanessa discuss art and literature and agree that on these subjects: *there is no one like KM* [Katherine Mansfield] *or* [Morgan] *Forster even with whom it's worth discussing one's business.*[37] Vanessa had been reading *The Waves* for three days and is so enthralled she is left breathless.

I can understand Vanessa's breathlessness; the writing is as rich as poetry, the scenes so vivid, the theme so condensed that it is a drain on the head and the emotions. It is a relief to turn to two former books and a simpler language: *Mrs Dalloway* 'Mrs Dalloway said she would buy the flowers herself.' Or *To the Lighthouse* 'Yes, of course, if it's fine tomorrow, said Mrs Ramsay. 'But you'll have to be up with the lark.'

In her biography, *Walter Sickert : A Conversation*, Virginia found herself grappling with difficulties, so Vanessa persuaded her to visit a retrospective exhibition of Sickert's work in Bond Street and Virginia noted: 'The life of the lower middle class interests him most – of innkeepers, shopkeepers, music-hall actors and actresses.' She admired the intimacy of his interiors with their attention to detail. The biography was published by the Hogarth Press in 1934.

In 1883 Walter Sickert was already familiar with St Ives, having previously been engaged with a party of actors. He talked to Vanessa about those days and remembered seeing her parents in the town, her father 'the most impressive personage in the area,' and her mother who 'had looked superb.' Sickert had a lifelong interest in theatre and had acted in Henry Irving's company of players when they toured Cornwall. The actor-manager Sir Henry Irving had been brought up by a Cornish aunt and had spent his boyhood years in Halsetown, a village just outside of St Ives. He was the first man to be knighted for services to the stage.

Opposite: Virginia's bedroom with tiles of Cornish Lugger and Lighthouse designed by Vanessa Bell

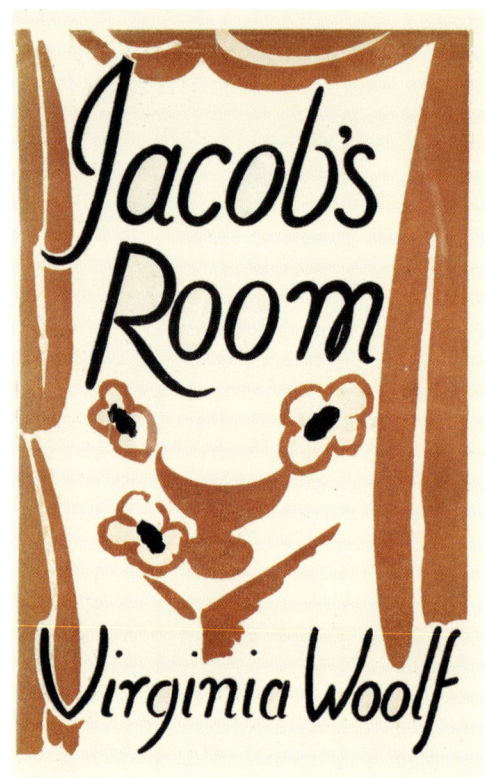

Dust jackets for Virginia's books

D H Lawrence's Tregerthen Cottage

Cottages at Zennor

Through Katherine Mansfield, Virginia learnt of three cottages that D H Lawrence had rented and were now for sale. She had not met Lawrence but remembers catching a glimpse of him in St Ives and knew of the controversy over his novels.

During the first world war, and in a burst of enthusiasm, D H Lawrence had persuaded Katherine Mansfield and John Middleton Murry to join him and Frieda in Tregerthen Cottage, Zennor, Cornwall, and live in the cottage next door : *Really, you must have the other place. .. I call it already Katherine's tower. ..It is only twelve strides from our house to yours: we can talk from the windows: and besides us, only the gorse, and the fields, the lambs skipping and hopping like anything, and seagulls fighting with the ravens, and sometimes a fox, and a ship on the sea.*[38]

In April 1916 Katherine and Murry responded to his call and occupied the Tower House, next to the Lawrence's. However, Katherine couldn't tolerate the rages and battles that Lawrence and Frieda indulged in, when they were literally fighting; or even the loving and playful times, when Lawrence was taking up Frieda's breakfast in bed. Katherine and Murry escaped to Mylor and shortly afterwards back to London.

In 1919, at Katherine Mansfield's coaxing, Virginia took the lease of the three cottages at Tregerthen for which the owner, Captain Short, charged £5 a year each. However, Virginia and Leonard neither visited nor stayed there. Meanwhile, they had found their ideal house in Sussex and Monk's house became their permanent home.

Katherine Mansfield had idealized the cottages to Virginia and the valley running down to the sea covered in primroses, violets and bluebells but in fact she found her cottage cold and the surroundings of stone and moor uninspiring. In May 1916 Katherine writes in a letter to Beatrice

The Tower House and Tregerthen Cottage from Eagle's Nest

Monk's House

Opposite: Portrait of Virginia Woolf by Vanessa Bell 1912

Campbell: *Today I can't see a yard, thick mist and rain and a tearing wind with it. Everything is faintly damp. The floor of the tower is studded with Cornish pitchers catching the drops. Except for my little maid [who she calls the Cornish Pasty] I am alone, for Murry and Lawrence have plunged off to St Ives with rucksacks on their backs and Frieda is in her cottage . . I feel I and the Cornish Pasty had drifted out to sea - and would never be seen again.*[39] Katherine couldn't write in Zennor. But Lawrence, who loved the gorse and heather and rugged landscape found it ideal for his writing.

Lawrence Accused of Spying

During 1916/1917 Lawrence had written *Women in Love* in Cornwall, his sequel to *The Rainbow*. This novel received as much notoriety as *The Rainbow* because of its overt sexuality. It was published in America in 1920, but before this time, 1917, Lawrence and Frieda were escorted to St Ives railway station by the police and put on a train to London. They were accused of being German spies, quite understandably, as far as the Cornish were concerned; Frieda was German and her relative was Baron Von Richthofen, the fighter pilot known as the Red Baron, an ace flyer who shot down a great number of English planes and was the target of the Allies pilots who wanted the accolade of finishing off the exploits of the Red Baron. There were also a number of merchant ships sunk between St Ives and Land's End at this time. The Lawrence's were thought to be signalling to the enemy by showing lights from their cottage windows to waiting submarines.

Enemies, Friends and Admirers

Virginia Woolf, although a controversial figure, a harsh critic, a cruel judge of other people, a mad genius, a beauty, a woman of wit and observation; she is all and more, but it is perhaps best that she is viewed from the perspective of people who were ambivalent about her and were forgiving of her temperament and were at various times enemies, friends and admirers.

Perhaps the truest picture of Virginia comes through the eyes of a sixteen year old 'factotum' working at the Hogarth Press in 1928, Richard Kennedy. He had a personal relationship with the fiery and exacting Leonard and quietly observed Virginia at work:

She looks at us over the top of her steel-rimmed spectacles, her grey hair hanging over her forehead and a shag cigarette hanging from her lips. She wears a hatchet-blue overall and sits hunched in a wicker armchair with her pad on her knees and a small typewriter beside her. Leonard was like a magician, who kept them all going 'by his strength of will.' Mrs W is a beautiful doll, very precious, but sometimes rather uncontrollable. Perhaps like the doll, she hasn't got a soul [40]

VIRGINIA WOOLF

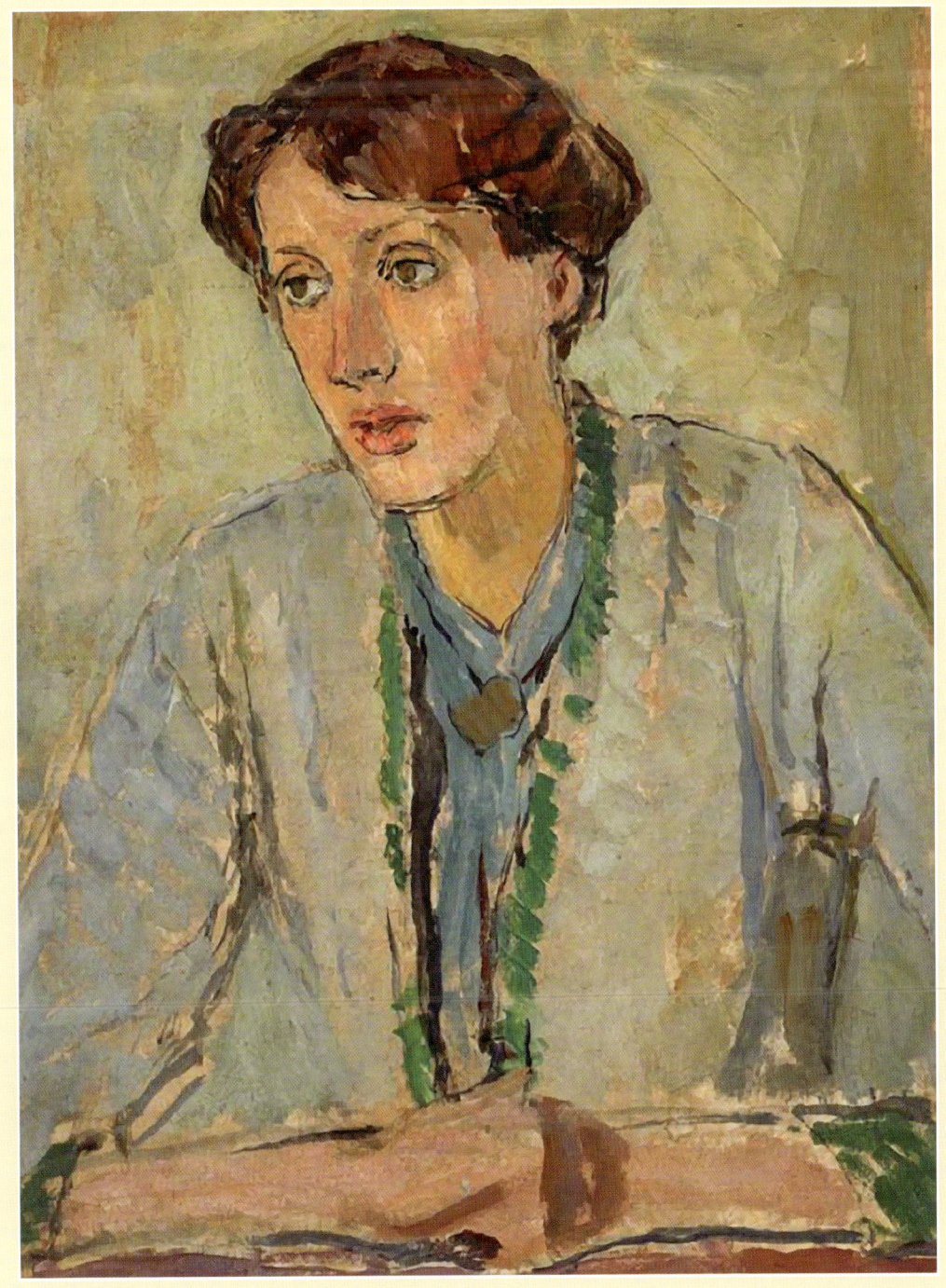

In spite of the many biographies and studies on Virginia, this book, with its evocative drawings, is the most intimate portrait of the woman we think we all know through her own diaries and journals. Richard Kennedy finally sums her up: *I think she is rather cruel in spite of the kind rather dreamy way she looks at you.*[40a]

However, that is a male point of view from a working relationship. From a personal friendship the picture shows a different Virginia. Katherine Mansfield in a letter to Virginia, April 1919 writes: *I have burned to write to you ever since you were here last. The East Wind made my journey in the train an impossibility; it set up ponds and pools in my left lung wherein the Germs and the Toxins – two families I detest – bathed and refreshed themselves and flourished and multiplied*[41].

In the same month Katherine writes again, and here you see the rivalry, and the admiration, that existed between these two remarkable writers: *Virginia, I have read your article on Modern Novels. You write so* damned *well, so* devilish *well. But I positively must see you soon. I want to talk over so much.*[42] Virginia confided to her diary after Katherine's death that she was jealous of her writing but that they had something in common, 'which I shall never find in anyone else.'

Dora Carrington writing to Gerald Brenan in April 1923 states: *You can't be too enthusiastic, to please me, over Virginia! I always feel she is one of the few people it has actually been tremendously good fortune to have known in this life. I am sure few women since the beginning of the world have equalled her for wit and charm, and a special rare kind of beauty.*[43] On a visit to Tidmarsh, to see Leonard and Virginia, September 1923, she writes to Gerald Brenan: *I like the Woolves far more than they like me. Ugh. I have a queer love for Virginia which fills me with emotion when I see her. They talk better than any people I know.*[44]

Virginia was the last person to see Carrington alive and, spending the day with her, she was full of sympathy, understanding and affection for her and her grief over the death of Lytton Strachey with whom Carrington lived at Tidmarsh, along with her husband, Ralph Partridge. The next day, 11th March 1932, they heard of Carrington's death from an accidental shotgun wound, although she had previously tried to kill herself while Lytton was dying of cancer. Virginia committed suicide in 1941, after several earlier attempts. She drowned herself in the River Ouse.

A satisfactory and pleasing portrait of Virginia Woolf comes from a letter written by Dora Carrington.

'How quickly the conversation becomes intelligent and amusing when Virginia talks!' [45]

Vanessa

I cannot remember a time when Virginia did not mean to be a writer, and I a painter.[1]

Vanessa Stephen had an early introduction to Cornwall. She breathed the Cornish air before she could barely walk and talk. In a letter dated May 18th, 1879 at the imminent birth of his first child by Julia, Leslie Stephen wrote:

I only hope that it will be of the right sex i.e. the feminine, as I need hardly say. I like some particular boys; but the genus boy seems to me one of nature's mistakes. Girls improve as they grow up; but the boy generally deteriorates.[2]

He must therefore have been delighted when Vanessa was born on May 30th. He went on to say he had a good pair of boys in his stepsons [George and Gerald]. Soon after the birth the Stephens planned a holiday trip to Cornwall and Leslie remarked that Vanessa was flourishing and Julia fully recovered.

By the autumn of 1881 Leslie Stephen wrote to his American friend Charles Eliot Norton that he had bought a house at St Ives:

The children will be able to run straight out of the house to a lovely bit of sand and have good air and quiet. But it makes me feel more than ever that my locomotive powers are getting terribly hampered. With six children hanging on to my skirts, I have little hope of ever getting farther away than Cornwall, except in imagination.[3]

The children, whether in Hyde Park Gate or at Talland House, were never in neglect of their education. Although they had no formal schooling, the Stephen parents were both teachers to their second young family. Stella records: *Mother gave Adrian an hour's lessons.* In the absence of Julia, Leslie wrote to tell her: *The little ones were very good: all 3 sitting on my knee to look at the bear book &*

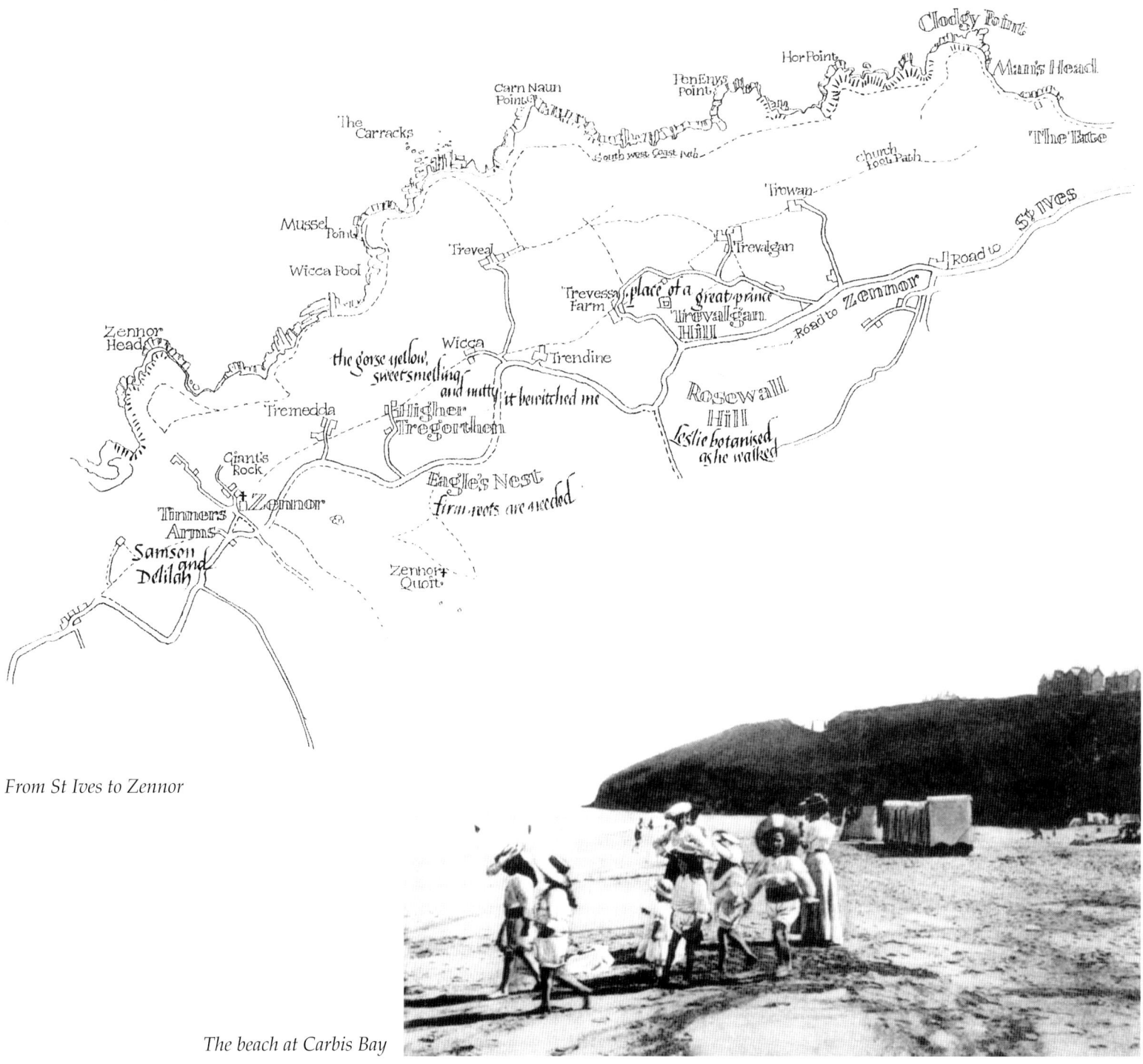

From St Ives to Zennor

The beach at Carbis Bay

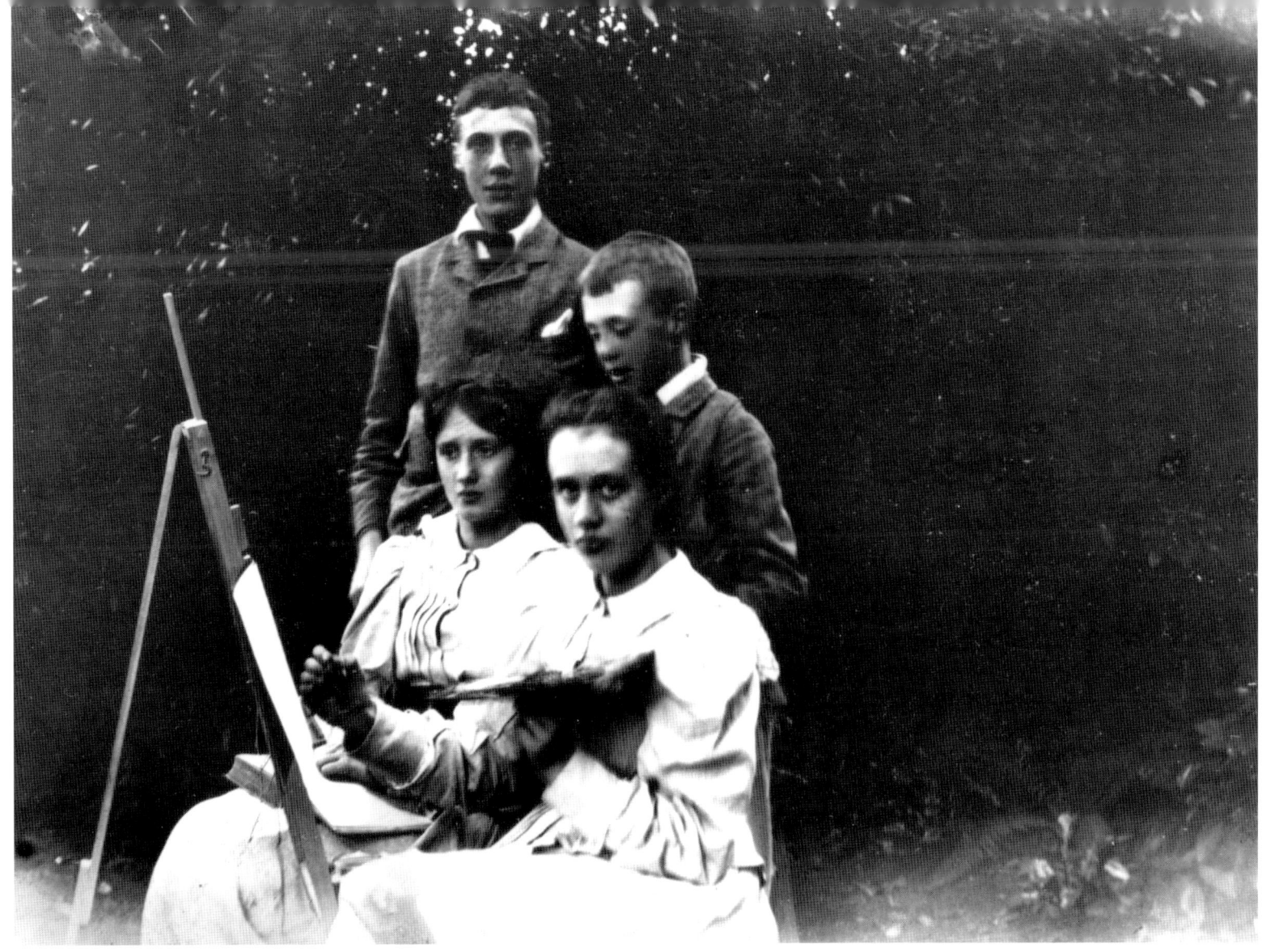

listening whilst Nessa explained with great elocution what you were to do if you met a wild beast in a wood.[4] The following day he wrote again.

Vanessa, Virginia, Thoby, Adrian

I had my lunch & saw Nessa do her letters – like a flash of lightning. In fact, she clearly knows them perfectly now, when she chooses, little puss.[5]

Virginia, at a young age, recognized in her sister a passion for art: *Once I saw her scrawl on a black door a great maze of lines, with white chalk. "When I am a famous painter - " she began, and then turned shy and rubbed it out in her capable way.*[6] Stella's St Ives diary of 1893 is full of such entries as: *Nessa Mother & I settled down to paint etc. in Rose garden. - Nessa & I sat in garden, she painted I worked.*[7]

Lanham's Workshop

During those childhood years, Vanessa was painting in watercolour and grappling with the difficulties of drawing. The environment began shaping her thoughts and ideas. She was aware that a colony of artists lived in the small town: . *that the sea was beautiful and might be painted some day, and perhaps once or twice she looked steadily in the glass when no one was by and saw a face that excited her strangely, her being began to have a definite shape, a place in the world.*[8]

A Walk into St Ives

Even in so small a town as St Ives, sketch pads and paints were available because of the proliferation of artists. Vanessa and Virginia used to visit Lanham's shop and gallery, where artists displayed their paintings and Whistler had once asked James Lanham: *Why don't you start selling paints. I have to send all the way to Cambridge for my paints.*[9] Virginia remembered they would: *go down to the town and buy penny boxes of tintacks or whatever it might be at Lanham's.*[10]

James Lanhams shop

Below left: *Fore Street 1900s*

Below right: *Fore Street 2014*

Fisher Girl *by H Harewood Robinson*

Stella noted in her diary of 1893: *M[other] & I went to town saw the pictures. B[ought] none & odds & ends & met the others returning from sail.'* On another visit to the gallery they were *'very much struck by a picture by Mrs Robinson.'*[11] And Stella took a photograph of a painting by Mr Robinson.

During the thirteen years and long months of childhood in those summer days at Talland House, Vanessa's trips into town would have taken her past the painter Louis Grier's studio on the harbour front. The sea lapped the net lofts, boat builders, and cottages at its edge, before Wharf Road was built in 1922. The artist's many friends would be capturing sunrise or sunset in paint, the lighthouse on Smeaton's pier, or boats as they sailed out in the bay to the fishing grounds. Louis Grier was a favourite among the fishermen and the butt of their jokes.

Of his Nocturnes, they said he couldn't row out fast enough to catch the sun as it went down.

A Volunteer for the Lifeboat *by Maria Robinson 1892*

Louis Grier's Studio – centre

Low Tide, St Ives by Louis Grier

Harbour by Moonlight
by Hayley Lever

STUDIOS

Vanessa would know of the many sail lofts used as studios, as she strolled in Downalong, the epicentre of the fishing community, its harsh life and work. The influx of artists into the town during the 1880s meant a proliferation of premises rented out as studios to supplement the fishermen's income from the dwindling fishing industry. Some boasted skylights and were large enough to live in. The best and largest of the converted sail lofts lined the Atlantic beach. These were Porthmeor, Piazza and Barnaloft and during spring tides the studios would be swamped, not only by gigantic seas, but by mountains of sand pressing against the huge windows. Piazza and Barnaloft studios have since been demolished and replaced by holiday flats.

Vanessa would have noticed that the artists were ladies and gentlemen, setting up their easels and canvas to paint their seascapes. Every year there would be Show Day. The art critic, Lewis Hind, wrote: *More pictures are painted in Cornwall in the course of the year than in any county. The great centres*

Porthmeor Studios before and after renovation, completed in 2012.

are Newlyn, St Ives and Falmouth, and the votes of the Cornish contingent, it is said, can turn the scale in an election at the Royal Academy.[12]

Many of these artists visited Talland House: *Mr & Mrs Titcomb to tea*. The Titcombs lived at Windy Parc and Stella notes: *Father and Mr M. to Titcombs then for a walk*. Titcomb painted the fishermen at their work on the harbour. *Mrs A Stokes & Mrs Birch to tea*.[13] This would be the artist Marianne Stokes and the other could have been the wife of the artist Lamorna Birch, living in Lamorna Valley. Vanessa may even have met the Finnish artist, Helene Schjerfbeck, now among the foremost artists of that country and friend of Marianne Stokes. The two women had studied together in Europe and often painted the same subject matter and used the same models, as in *The Convalescent*. The girl was probably a child from the fishing community.

Virginia Woolf & Vanessa Bell - A CHILDHOOD IN ST IVES

Charles and Ruth Simpson with students

Artists and Onlookers

Top left: The Convalescent
by Helene Schjerfbeck

Top right: The Cottage
by W H Y Titcomb

Painting en Plein Air

Ten miles away at Newlyn, a fishing village beyond the town of Penzance, other fishing families were accommodating artists. At Newlyn Vanessa would have met Walter Langley, the first major artist to settle there and record with his brush the lives of the fisherfolk. Stanhope and Elizabeth Forbes were prominent among the artists. Elizabeth was renowned for her paintings of children and spent much time painting in Percy Craft's studio in St Ives, which she preferred to Newlyn. Stanhope's *Fish Sale on a Cornish Beach*, exhibited at the Royal Academy in 1885, and *The Health of the Bride* shown in 1889, did much to put Newlyn at the forefront of artists painting in this genre. In 1899 at their home, Higher Faughan, the Forbes established the Newlyn School, famous for paintings of uncompromising realism.

Painting *en plein air* was the newest development in Britain, but it was already prominent in France and Brittany, where artists from Newlyn and St Ives had been influenced by this technique.

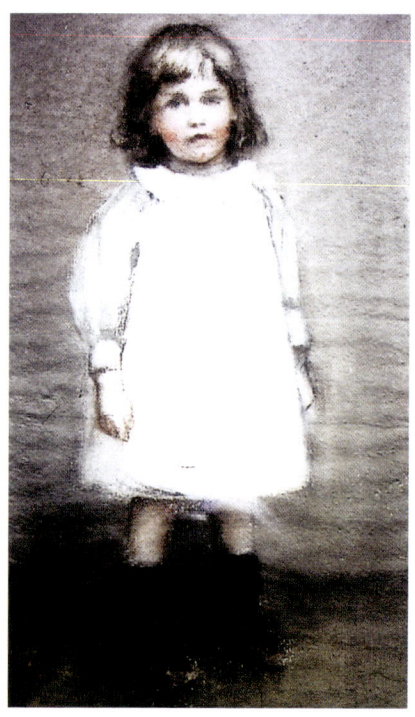

Above: Mary Dow
by Thomas Millie Dow

Right: A Mariner's Sunday School, Fore Street
by W H Y Titcomb

Norman Garstin, renowned for his atmospheric painting of Penzance promenade in 1889 *The Rain it Raineth Every Day* wryly remarked that a painting could not be good unless the artist had caught a cold doing it. This work is owned by the Penzance Charter Trustees and exhibited at Penlee House Museum and Art Gallery.

In Newlyn artists were using local models, posed in a cottage or on the beach *en plein air*, amid fish and boats, or creating some dramatic scene of distraught and exhausted women, looking out to sea, where dawn offers no hope of a sail or the return of their menfolk, nor the boat on which their livelihood depended. St Ives also depicted scenes in cottage interiors, where the narrative is clearly told.

Titcomb captures the very essence of Methodism in his depiction of scenes from this strict faith, but there is also belief in this religion held and practiced by the local population. Vanessa would have been familiar with the artists' portrayal of the inhabitants of St Ives, whereas when she travelled on the continent the paintings and artists would be so different and far ahead of anything Britain was producing at this time.

Julius Olsson in his Porthmeor Studio

Show Day and Julius Olsson

In St Ives the main subject of the paintings was the landscape and the sea in all its changing moods. At the yearly Show Day the population of the town and local schools and hoards of incoming visitors traipsed round the studios to see the paintings, which were destined for judgement by the committee at the Royal Academy. Pictures were framed, packed and transported by the Great Western Railway from Lanham's Gallery to the Royal Academy or Paris Salon. The peak of achievement was to be hung 'on the line' (at eye level) at the RA Summer Exhibition, to be seen by thousands, and perhaps to capture the attention of members of the Chantrey Bequest, who were buying paintings and sculpture to form the nucleus of a National Collection. Vanessa attended the Summer Shows at the RA, where she would recognize the names of many St Ives artists and as a child would have visited their studios. Indeed, Mr and Mrs Julius Olsson were friends of the Stephen family at Talland House.

In 1911 Olsson's seascape painting *Moonlit Shore* was bought by the Chantrey Bequest for the nation. His paintings were accepted to hang in the Royal Academy 175 times. He was elected a Royal Academician in 1920. Olsson, together with Louis Grier, set up the first School of Landscape and Marine Painting in St Ives in 1895. The advertisement for their school appeared in the St Ives *Weekly Summary*:

Two young artists Mr Louis Grier and Mr Julius Olsson, are announcing the opening in St Ives, Cornwall, of a School of Landscape and Marine Painting. The main idea of this School is to give students an opportunity of studying out of door effects, and therefore the work of students will, weather permitting, be carried on

Visitors to a St Ives studio.

Moonlight St Ives *Bay Julius Olsson*

Julius Olsson

Borlase Smart

actually in the open air, and will only be taken into the studio when atmospheric conditions render open air painting impossible.[14]

Olsson's studio fronted the Atlantic coast with its huge seas and rolling surf. He was described in *The Studio* magazine as 'a big man with a big heart, who paints big pictures with big brushes in a big studio.'

Borlase Smart

In 1913 the artist, Borlase Smart, keen to live and work among artists in St Ives, came to study seascape painting with the master, Julius Olsson. Unfortunately, the First World War interrupted these studies and his desire to live in St Ives. Smart joined the army at the first opportunity and was a Captain in the Artists' Rifles. He was troubled by the devastation of the countryside in which

St Ives Bay *Borlase Smart*

he fought and appointed himself an unofficial war artist. He drew and recorded the destruction of the villages and towns of France and on the Somme. Many of his drawings are in the Imperial War Museum. He had worked as art correspondent for the Western Morning News in Plymouth for ten years and knew the importance of news. In 1919 Borlase Smart fulfilled his ambition to live in St Ives and brought his young wife, Irene, to Ocean Wave Studio where they set up home, having a canvas sail to divide working and living areas.

Sickert and Whistler

During the Stephens' long association with St Ives Walter Richard Sickert came to the town, when Vanessa was only five and he, in 1884 at the age of twenty-three, was a student of James McNeill Whistler. They were lodging at Barnoon Terrace, with one of the best views over the town and bay. Later, Vanessa came to admire Sickert's paintings, and he was very encouraging in her early years as a painter. Sickert, among other artist friends, floated on the edges of the Bloomsbury Group. Virginia observed: *the intimacy that exists in Sickert's pictures between his people and their rooms. The bed, the chest of drawers, the one picture and the vase on the mantelpiece are all expressive of the owner.*[15] In time Vanessa would encapsulate all these features in her paintings of her own environment.

In St Ives Sickert was mixing his master's paints, cleaning his brushes, and attending to his every whim and mood. Doubtless they sauntered into town and came upon artists struggling with their huge canvases whilst Whistler was painting on small wooden panels, the size of cigar box lids. Elizabeth Forbes was an admirer of both Whistler and Sickert, much to the annoyance of her husband.

Whistler was known for his nocturnes of the Thames, and seeing Louis Grier and his artist friends equally keen on producing effects of light and evening sunset on the harbour, probably dismissed their attempts, for it is well known that Whistler could not tolerate competition. Louis Grier wrote in ironic tone: *On fine nights the large doors at the end of the studio would be opened, and then we had a series of nocturnes that would have merited the artistic appreciation of Mr Whistler.*[16]

ART AND ARTISTS

Virginia kept an account of Vanessa's progress to achieve her goals in art and noted she was reading Ruskin's *The Elements of Drawing* and following its instructions. Vanessa and Virginia were furthering their art education by frequent visits to the Royal Academy and other art galleries. In 1897 they saw the exhibition of Lord Leighton's paintings and next day at the National Gallery: *We saw everything – old Italians, Dutches, English and a great room full of Turner water colours.*[17] A few days later they paid a visit to the New Gallery, Regent Street, which was exhibiting George Frederic Watts's paintings in celebration of his eightieth birthday.

Arthur Hayward painting outside the Arts Club

The artist had lived for over twenty years at Little Holland House, Kensington, the home of Julia Stephen's aunt. Ottoline Morrell described Vanessa: *as beautiful as a Watts painting*, which is unfortunate because Vanessa had little regard for Watts as a painter. She considered he had wasted his talent: *neglecting the art of painting and using it only as a half-learned language.*[18] The remark is typical of the art student who wishes to push the boundaries of art to reflect the spirit of the time.

The sisters attempted to instruct girls less fortunate than themselves, namely a group of six working women, meeting them on the steps of the National Gallery and taking them: *laboriously through the Early Italians . . . how far pictures are intelligible to them – I don't know. It is hard work.*[19]

As well as their walks in Kensington Gardens, the sisters often took bus trips up to Hampstead, where they had contact with many other painters and writers. It was here that Vanessa visited Mark Gertler in his Hampstead studio; eight years after he had finished his studies at the Slade. She told Ottoline Morrell: *He's painting a great picture of a merry-go-round* [now owned by the Tate] *but he won't let us see it till it's finished. He came to lunch the other day and was very amusing and intelligent. I liked him, and he's so interested in his painting he can hardly talk of anything else, which I rather like.*[20] On Hampstead Heath, 'this little vision of country,' Vanessa and Virginia could tramp for miles over the heath, and from the highest point at Whitestone Pond, they could look out over London and beyond to the Surrey hills.

Vanessa was having lessons from Margaret Flower, a painter, who instructed her in art history by visiting the various galleries. At the Grafton Gallery in 1897 they saw the work of Ford Madox Brown and had the good fortune to meet William Holman Hunt, who talked about the paintings. William, a member of the Pre-Raphaelite Brotherhood, had first visited Cornwall in 1860 with the painter Val Prinsep, a relative of Julia Stephen. Vanessa was familiar with Hunt's son, Hilary, born the same year as Vanessa, and his sister Gladys, from the days when they too, spent summer holidays in St Ives and played in the garden at Talland House.

1897 was a good year for artists in St Ives, thirty of whom had their work accepted and hung in the Annual Summer Exhibition at the RA. It was reported in the local paper: *The old town by the Cornish sea is represented in every room in Burlington House. We cannot doubt that St Ives will now be more firmly established than ever as the most successful and popular Art resort in the West of England.*[21]

Judging the Pictures at The Royal Academy 1894

The Royal Academy School

Vanessa's experience of the rich and fertile grounding in art as a child in St Ives, where there was 'an artist on every corner,' must have given her confidence in her own ability to succeed as a painter. In 1901 she applied to study at the Royal Academy School. She wrote to her brother Thoby: *I have been at the studio all today where I am drawing my Academy figure. It's very dull and I'm doing it very badly, so I don't expect I shall even get my first drawings accepted. I don't know where I shall hide my head then.*[22] But her drawings were good enough and she was accepted. Later she was to despise the RA's staid, traditional, Victorian, and unchanging attitude to modern art.

Following this success, she submitted the drawings for a competition at her old school, Mr Cope's School of Art in South Kensington, and was awarded a medal. On three days a week Vanessa left Virginia to her reading and studies, and bicycled off in a large floppy hat and a long skirt. She rarely missed a day. Cope's school was geared to training students for entry to the Royal Academy. The RA Schools had for the past ten years allowed women students to study 'from the partially draped female figure'. The probationary year was a test to 'weed out' the less capable candidates:

The first advantage will be the exclusion of the ordinary run of the lady students, as only the best of them will be equal to the new and more painter-like test. For those of them who succeed in the preliminary examination the new regulation – that of permitting them to study flesh-painting from the semi-nude – is a boon.[23]

Leslie Stephen writes with pride to a relation in 1902: *The chief event of this week is that Nessa has been passed into the upper school of the Academy. It is good because, I fancy, she was getting rather bored with the eternal drawing from casts & will now have to paint some heads.*[24] Only the best of the female students passed their probationary year and many of her special friends failed. One of these was Margery Snowden [known as Snow], who remained a lifelong correspondent and admiring friend. Vanessa practiced portraiture on Margery, although these seem not to have survived. In the best tradition of students of art, Vanessa continued to study paintings and attend exhibitions.

Leslie is pleased that interest has been shown in Vanessa and that someone has spoken well of her drawing. 'I shall be truly glad if she has a talent that way.' Although Leslie has no particular interest in painting: *I have always been shy with artistic people, who inhabit a world very unfamiliar to me.*[25] He accompanied Vanessa and the children, willingly, to art exhibitions: *Us four Stella and father went to the National Portrait Gallery…and we went on to the National Gallery.*[26] Vanessa enjoyed studying for three years at the Royal Academy Schools from 1901-1904. She wrote to her friend Margery:

[John Singer] *Sargent is teaching most extraordinarily well at the RA. How I wish you were there. . . He insists upon thick paint and makes one try get the right tone at once – apparently the drawing is to be got entirely by painting thickly the different tones. The one thing he is down upon is when he thinks anyone is trying for an effect regardless of truth.*[27]

Even mild-mannered Sargent, visiting, Professor at the RA, had crushed and 'subdued' several of the women students by his criticism.

A Brief Study at the Slade

After completing her studies at the Royal Academy Vanessa applied to study at the Slade School of Drawing, Painting and Sculpture. Here she met Philip Wilson Steer, Professor Frederick Brown, and Professor Henry Tonks, who regarded it almost as a duty to scare off the number of females anxious to study with them: *Of course there are many minor lights whom he* [Tonks] *squashes I don't think anyone has had any praise.*[28]

As a child at Talland House, Vanessa was unaware that some of her future tormentors of her student days at the Slade School of Art, Frederick Brown and Philip Wilson Steer, were in St Ives. They were staying at Chy-an-Porth, opposite the Porthminster Hotel, the home of the local artist Moffat Lindner, whose paintings of Venice and St Ives seascapes were closer to Impressionism than many of his St Ives contemporaries.

While in St Ives Steer painted a portrait of Lindner's wife Augusta. She was also a painter, and came to St Ives to study under Julius Olsson, but gave up when her husband's work commanded more favourable attention from the critics.

The Slade had opened in 1871 and was run by practicing artists who placed emphasis on working from the figure, as in the French *ateliers*. There was a Women's Life Room, where studies were made of draped models who posed every day, and in fact they also had mixed life classes.

Vanessa noted a young man of seventeen whom she marked down as promising. He was Mark Gertler: He studied at the Slade in 1908. Vanessa prophesied, *I think he may be going to be good*, He fell in love with an elusive fellow student, Dora Carrington. Other students at this time were Paul Nash, Stanley Spencer and Ben Nicholson.

Painting of Augusta Lindner by Philip Wilson Steer

Staff and students at a Slade School of Art Picnic c.1912. Back row: unknown, unknown, David Bomberg, Fred Brown, Charles Koe Child (Secretary of the Slade), Muirhead Bone (?), Second row: Isaac Rosenberg (kneeling), unknown, Dorothy Meyer, Dorothy Brett, Ka Cox, unknown, unknown, unknown, unknown. Front row: Dora Carrington, Barbara Hines, Richard Nevison, Mark Gertler, Edward Wadsworth, Adrian Allinson, Stanley Spencer, unknown.

Henry Tonks succeeded Fred Brown as Professor of Fine Art at the Slade where previously he taught Vanessa. He was said to be 'the most formidable teacher of his generation.'

WOMEN PAINTERS

At one time women students outnumbered men. Two important contemporary women painters who had also studied at the Slade were Gwen John in 1895 and Dora Carrington in 1910. There were also Sylvia Frances Milman, Winifred Knights, Ethel Walker, Nina Hamnett, Iris Tree, Dorothy Brett, Barbara Hiles-Bagenal. There, too, were Dod Procter, who afterwards studied and lived in Newlyn, and Marjorie Mostyn who, with her husband Leonard Fuller established a School of Painting in St Ives in 1938.

Henry Tonks had taught, or rather 'squashed', Vanessa. She also felt intimidated by artists of the New English Art Club, whose members all seemed to have: *the secret of the universe within their grasp, a secret one was not worthy to learn, especially if one was that terrible low creature, a female painter.*[29] In the early years of the twentieth century it was still difficult for females to get an art education; training was simplest for the daughters of artists, who were familiar with a studio and not so intimidated in this man's world.

One other connection with Vanessa's student days was the tall slender figure of Bernard Leach. In 1903 Leach became a student at the Slade, during the few months when Vanessa was there. Did they ever meet, I wonder? - although I learn from Vanessa's writing that she *made no friends there and soon left*.[30]

A visit to Tate St Ives of former apprentice Leach Potters from New Zealand to USA . Far left is David Leach with Janet Leach seated

Bernard Leach

Bernard Leach studied drawing with Henry Tonks at the Slade, and etching with Frank Brangwyn at the London School of Art. Brangwyn was an early member of the colony, and among the first exhibitors in the new art gallery established by James Lanham in 1889.

In 1920 Bernard Leach, who had studied pottery in Japan, and his Japanese friend Shoji Hamada, established the Leach Pottery in St Ives, and rediscovered the craft of English slipware. They built the first Japanese climbing kiln in Europe. The Leach Pottery is a renowned place of pilgrimage

St Ives Harbour *by Alfred Wallis*

for students of ceramics from around the world. The artist, Patrick Heron, a conscientious objector during the Second World War, was invited by Bernard Leach to work at the Pottery.

Leach is responsible for the unique gravestone of Alfred Wallis, St Ives's most renowned primitive artist. Wallis, a semi-literate, retired fisherman, took up painting at the age of seventy. The quality of his paintings was recognised by Ben Nicholson and Christopher Wood when they walked past the old fisherman's cottage in Back Road West in 1928. Wallis's paintings now hang in the Tate Gallery, alongside those of Nicholson and Wood, without whose active promotion, the old man would have died in obscurity with other poor and primitive artists of his class.

Vanessa began her studies at the Slade but by January 1905 she had decided she was wasting her time. She had, after all, completed her training at the Royal Academy and wanted to move on, rather than repeat the process. However, in spite of complaining of the various knocks she received to her confidence by the harshness of Henry Tonks, surprisingly, she invited him to her studio at Gordon Square to view and criticise her paintings. After some time he did arrive, and Virginia noted the nervousness of Vanessa waiting for him 'in great misery' to pass judgement, which he did with a good deal of severity but also 'some praise'.

Bernard Leach tiles on Alfred Wallis' grave

Vanessa was also keen to obtain a critique from John Singer Sargent, her former tutor, whose studio she visited, and who remembered her from the RA Schools. He was a Royal Academician and a renowned portrait painter of the rich, famous and aristocratic. Vanessa must indeed have trembled at his approach.

Vanessa Avoids being the Angel in the House

When Vanessa took over the management of the house at Hyde Park Gate, after the deaths of her mother in 1895 and her stepsister Stella two years later, she was beset by family and domestic problems. Leslie was in his sixties when Vanessa, at eighteen, was forced to assume household responsibilities. Her father took a bully's delight in trying to terrify Vanessa over the household accounts, as though punishing her for not being her mother, or Stella – the ideal models of womanhood. Vanessa was stoic and resilient while Virginia was moved to silent fury at the injustice of their father's treatment of Vanessa; but summer visitors to Talland House, and especially her cousin Herbert Fisher, had a different view: *Leslie, so formidable within the home, was a different creature when he was striding over the Cornish cliffs, botanizing as he went, repeating poetry, and overflowing with good spirits and enjoyment. I learnt to know him from these St Ives visits and always held him in deep affection and regard.*[31]

An artists' cricket team. Stanhope Forbes, standing, third from right

Vanessa must have looked back to those carefree childhood years in St Ives, when her main social duty was entertaining her parents' many visitors to Talland House, often taking them down to Porthminster beach. Their life was recorded by Stella in her diary of 1893: *Lovely bathing. Adrian swam quite a good way. Nessa & I painted honeysuckle in Rose Garden,*[32] *'Children and I blackberried . . came back late for tea to find Dick & Rupert* [Brooke] *waiting for cricket.'*. Not only were the children mad about cricket but the Newlyn and St Ives artists were always in competition in the game. Vanessa would have been familiar with most of these artists.

Vanessa fulfilled her new role, as housekeeper, reluctantly. The practicalities of life must have overwhelmed her, especially with the extra demands made upon her by a demanding father and Virginia's nervous breakdown; but she had her escape route, her art. It was indeed art, which Vanessa doggedly followed when expected to be 'the Angel in the House', that saved her from being tied to the life of self-sacrifice demanded by Victorian society:

When I got into the grubby, shabby, dirty world of art students . . . I wanted nothing else in the way of society. They were separate entirely from my home life and so a great relief . . . in their company one could forget oneself and think of nothing but shapes and colours and the absorbing difficulties of oil paint.[33]

Hyde Park Gate, Kensington

Bloomsbury

After the death of her father, Vanessa was free to move into the modern world and to make her own decisions without recourse to him, or her stepbrothers. From the constraints of her father's household Vanessa seems to have taken a giant leap into the new century. As decision-maker, in the years between 1897 and Leslie Stephen's death in 1904, she had learnt enough of household management to enable her to move the Stephen family from their home at Hyde Park Gate into the lighter, brighter house at 46 Gordon Square in Bloomsbury.

Here the four young people of the Stephen family, Thoby, Virginia and Adrian, under the direction of Vanessa, set about lightening the rooms in which they lived. The walls bounced light from pale colours and their faces shone into the room. Gone were the heavy William Morris wallpapers and sombre colours. Vanessa recalls the solemnity of Hyde Park Gate: *At dinner in the evening faces loomed out of the surrounding shade like Rembrandt portraits...*[34]

Vanessa took the family to Europe. In Venice they spent their mornings seeing pictures, and the afternoons churches. In Florence she bought old picture frames, very cheap, and nicer than any she could buy in London. In Paris they visited Rodin's studio and met many contemporary painters. It was in Paris that Vanessa came to know her brother Thoby's friend, Clive Bell.

Back to St Ives

In 1905 Vanessa, Virginia, Thoby and Adrian made a nostalgic and sentimental train journey back to their childhood home at St Ives. Vanessa was also escaping the attentions of Clive who had proposed to her for the second time. She wrote in a letter to her friend Margery:

When one is actually asked by a man to marry him, even though one has no feeling at all of that kind oneself, one is obliged to think rather more seriously about it than one has done before . . . I should be quite happy living with anyone whom I didn't dislike . . . if I could paint and lead the kind of life I like.[35]

Virginia tramped around the countryside in all weathers and Vanessa painted: *Vanessa, in Cornwall, painted several small seascapes, employing Whistler's method, using a red or brown base to deepen the blues of sea and sky.*[36] These paintings were perhaps lost in the bombing of the Fitzroy Street studio in 1940.

Vanessa wished her friend Margery could be with her in Cornwall. She wrote:

You can't imagine the colour of the sea here. It is quite unlike any other, and the country altogether is beautiful, very wild and bare. I mean to paint a great deal. I have established myself in my room much as we did in our hotels and mean to paint sunsets from the window. We look out across the bay, and the sun sets just behind the headland to the left, so that one gets most lovely effects on the sea.[37]

Now that Vanessa's painting career had begun, and with all the influences she gained from European artists, she seriously thought about her painting techniques and how they were to be achieved; should she paint thickly on a new canvas and try at once to achieve the right tone and colour, as advised by Sargent, or should she follow the example of Whistler and paint thinly, layer upon layer, building up to the final surface? This was a problem that engaged Vanessa's thoughts and in a lecture some years later she was to tell students: *It is indeed so exciting and so absorbing, this painters' world of form and colour, that once you are at its mercy you are in grave danger of forgetting all other aspects of the material world.*[38]

While in St Ives did Vanessa see the paintings of John Park and Hayley Lever? They were experimenting with Fauvism. They were briefly influenced by this new movement circulating in Paris for thick applications of paint, with heightened colour defining the subject matter. John Park's heavy impasto painting of the harbour is quite unlike his usual thin reflective, translucent colours.

The First Commission and the New English Art Club

Perhaps in opposition to the mainly literary predominance of the Thursday meetings in Gordon Square, Vanessa set up a society of painters known as the Friday Club, and within a month had organised their first exhibition and shown three of her paintings. Five years on the Friday Club was still operating.

Morning, West Pier St Ives, *1920s*
John Park

St Ives Harbour,
Hayley Lever

Vanessa finally left her student days behind with her first exhibition in 1905 at the New Gallery, London, at which she showed her first commissioned portrait of Nelly [Lady Cecil]. The four Stephen children visited the exhibition many times to celebrate Vanessa's success.

The following year Vanessa was engaged to paint the portrait of Lord Robert, and a further commission from a Mrs Seton to paint portraits of her children. The New Gallery at which Vanessa exhibited her work was none other than the New English Art Club, which she had railed against when she was a student, for their superior attitude.

William Henry Bartlett, Henry Scott Tuke and Thomas Cooper Gotch, three artists associated with St Ives, Falmouth and Newlyn, proposed the founding of the new English Art Club in 1886. Others were Frederick Brown, John Singer Sargent and W J Laidlay, who was their first chairman. Other St Ives artist members were Thomas Millie Dow, Henry Detmold, Adrian Stokes, Marianne Stokes, Sir Alfred East, Julius Olsson, William Holt Yates Titcomb, and Moffat Lindner. In the early years the painters felt they had joined an egalitarian society in which members possessed no privileges of rank; work was judged and accepted on its merits, without personal bias or the chancy competition of the Royal Academy. Vanessa was exhibiting in the same gallery as more recognized and established artists, among them John Singer Sargent.

Vanessa Marries

Vanessa was preoccupied with Clive's persistence in pursuing her with his proposal of marriage. She asked him to 'go away for a year.' He spent some time at his family home, engaging in the hunting, shooting and fishing activities so despised by Vanessa. However, fate pointed circumstances in Clive's direction when in 1906 her beloved brother Thoby died. They had returned to Gordon Square from a trip to Greece; both were ill, but while Vanessa recovered, Thoby died of typhoid fever. He was 26.

Clive and Vanessa consoled each other over this death, united in their grief through their love of Thoby, and one feels Vanessa accepted Clive's third proposal of marriage in a desperate effort to evade the spectre of death that had pursued her in the last few years. Also, she could talk endlessly about Thoby, one of Clive's closest friends.

Vanessa and Clive married at St Pancras Registry Office in February 1907, and went at once to Paris. From Paris Vanessa wrote to her friend Margery: *we have asked a young artist called Duncan Grant to dine with us. We both knew him before we came here as he is a cousin of the Stracheys.*

*He is clever and very nice. I hope we shall see him in London quite often when he goes back there.*³⁹ This would appear to be the first stirrings of Vanessa's attraction to Duncan Grant. It also proved a difficult time for Vanessa. She had not been able to paint since her brother's death, but informed Margery: *Now I mean to have models and work hard at painting some nudes and perhaps one or two portraits.* ⁴⁰

In March 1909 Vanessa wrote to Virginia from the Lizard, in Cornwall. She described the countryside on their walks and the effects of light breaking through a grey sky, and how the subject would be tackled by various painters and how they would have portrayed the scene, but her attempts to capture the moment were disappointing to her: *I flattered myself that I saw how it ought to be treated but I could not do it. A melancholy watercolour of a sunset is my only achievement.*⁴¹ Later, at Cleeve House, Clive's family home, Vanessa was cast down by the family's inability to talk of nothing but the weather, or dogs and shooting. She deplored their dull conversation and wasting their lives doing nothing. In such tedious company she felt 'clever and almost a genius.' She found it impossible to paint in such an arid atmosphere and envied Virginia: *what is one to do in Wiltshire while you are sniffing the smells of St Ives?* ⁴² However, Clive's privileged background in terms of not having to earn money to live, and her own fortunate financial circumstances, made a comfortable living possible, where they could travel, employ servants and develop whatever creative talents they possessed.

By September 1909 Vanessa was at Studland Bay, near Poole Harbour, in more invigorating company. She had invited Lytton Strachey to join them, and Virginia came too. This was one of a number of visits to Dorset which led to her producing one of her most ambitious and experimental works.

The painting *Studland Beach* is engaged with itself. Two seated figures in the foreground, with their backs to the onlooker, but looking very like Virginia and Vanessa's son Julian, sit watching a group on the edge of the sea, where four children are intent upon some occupation with the sand. A woman standing with her back to the viewer looks as though she is about to enter a canvas bathing tent, very like the Victorian tents on Porthminster beach in St Ives. Long swathes of colour sweep down from the left hand corner and give the painting an abstract quality, whilst there is also an obscure narrative element going on in the picture. Richard Shone described *Studland Beach, as one of the most radical paintings in England for its date.*⁴³

Studland Beach *1912 by Vanessa Bell*

Post-Impressionist Exhibitions 1910 and 1912

Roger Fry's exhibition of 1910, 'Manet and the Post-Impressionists,' at the Grafton Gallery caused shock waves through the art establishment. Fry predicted that he thought the show would be a 'great affair' and he was preparing himself 'for a huge campaign of outraged British Philistinism.' He was not wrong in his predictions. Vanessa was convinced that no other single exhibition had more effect on the younger generation of painters, and the shocking sensation experienced by the traditionalists only added to the fun and exhilaration: *That autumn of 1910 is to me a time when everything seemed springing to new life – a time when all was a sizzle of excitement, new relationships, new ideas, different and intense emotions all seemed crowding into one's life.*[44]

While Vanessa was thrilling to the opening up of everything in the art world, she was at the same time a worried mother. It was in 1910 that Quentin was born and failing to gain weight. Her friend Margery Snowden came for a month to help nurse Vanessa back to health and strength.

Vanessa was excited by the first Post-Impressionist Exhibition: *it was there I first saw a work by Cezanne, one that impressed me without my knowing why, of bare trees and house and water in front . . and I remember a very lovely little Van Gogh of flowers in a jug.*[45]

For Vanessa it was a sudden revelation and encouragement. The writer, Katherine Mansfield, felt similarly inspired and returned many times to view the Van Gogh paintings. This was all so new and stimulating.

Here the British public had the opportunity to view the work of Cezanne, Matisse, Picasso, Van Gogh, and Gauguin; painters who influenced Vanessa with their colourful and lyrical work. There were a few English painters she admired: Sickert, Augustus John, Steer and Sargent, but even then she thought their best work was behind them. At an exhibition in 1911 she expressed her opinion that Miss Gwen John was 'more interesting than anyone' but she felt the future of painting lay with the French artists.

ROGER FRY

During this time Vanessa and Roger Fry became close. She found him a stimulating and interesting companion. They could talk art and exchange ideas. He introduced her to the world of art dealers. Even then Roger realised the artist and designer in Vanessa and knew he could never achieve the lyrical compositions of her paintings. She did not return the compliment or admire his paintings. Fry was critic, appreciative admirer, entrepreneur, and someone who could move things forward by his enthusiasm and energy. He fell in love with Vanessa during the time he nursed her through a serious miscarriage in 1911, when she, Clive and Roger were travelling in Turkey.

Meanwhile, Clive was involved in his own affairs of the heart, and Duncan Grant was in a relationship with Vanessa's brother Adrian. In the free-thinking-and-acting circle of Bloomsbury, the frequency of mix and match partnerships was normal and occurred without critical disapproval.

For the second Post-Impressionist exhibition of 1912 Vanessa helped with the hanging, and noted there were thirty works of Matisse to be displayed, as well as works by Picasso. French, English and Russian artists were all represented. Vanessa exhibited three works, and Stanley Spencer, who later spent his honeymoon in St Ives but was then still a student, had his painting *John Donne Arriving in Heaven* selected and hung; this in defiance of Henry Tonks's advice to his students at the Slade to stay away from the contamination of the Grafton Gallery. Leonard Woolf, married to Virginia this same year, manned the exhibition and reported that large numbers of people came to the show: *nine out of ten of them either roared with laughter at the pictures or were enraged by them*.[46] However, Roger Fry expressed his pleasure that Professor Fred Brown, also of the Slade, had been converted to the ideas embodied in the paintings.

Lytton Strachey
by Vanessa Bell 1913

Vanessa's Painting Bought for the Nation

Vanessa was already well into her painting career by 1912, when she wrote to her husband: *Dearest, I have a most astonishing piece of news to give you. I have sold a picture! Doesn't that startle you? And you will be still more astonished when you hear who has bought it. The Contemporary Art Fund!* [47] The Contemporary Art Society purchased works by British artists, which were then given or loaned to public collections. The painting was *The Spanish Model* first exhibited along with three other of her pictures at the second Post-Impressionist exhibition. The visitors had come to the studio at 46 Gordon Square to purchase a specific work by Duncan Grant but as that painting was not available, they had chosen one of hers. This was incredible to Vanessa, who was ambivalent about her status as a professional artist. Her day, as with so many women, was broken up by important fragments of time with her two sons. She wrote from Asheham House, shared by Virginia with Vanessa and her family:

. . . I give Julian his reading lesson! . . . then I have to talk a little to Quentin, and then perhaps I paint, when curtain-making allows of it, but I haven't really embarked on much painting yet. Julian has lunch with me, which means that it takes about one-and-a-half hours, and I can't settle down to write letters after lunch, and then you see comes tea and the children again. [48]

Vanessa, in spite of her myriad duties to children and household, managed an active life of painting of canvases, murals, and decorative schemes, and exhibitions and travelling to Europe to study painting and meet other artists. In one of Vanessa's successful exhibitions she sold twelve pictures. She was amazed and thought it was largely because of an article in *The Times* written by art critic, Charles Marriott, one time resident in St Ives.

The Early Paintings of Vanessa

Vanessa's bold areas of colour in her 1911/12 painting *Virginia Woolf* show her quick, free use of the brush to provide outline, with infill blocks of colour. Features are hinted at. In a further study of 1912 *Virginia Woolf in a Deckchair*, there are no distinguishing facial features. With the merest of outlines for guidance, Vanessa uses her colour freely, fluidly and with confidence, especially so in *Lytton Strachey* 1913. She places her colour instinctively, dissolving form, enjoying laying the pigment on the canvas and exploring areas with her brush. It is a work in the style of the Fauvists. Her colleagues, Duncan Grant and Roger Fry, also painted Lytton at Asheham at this time but: *Bell's is by far the most vivid and successful painting, showing the future author in his Augustus John phase.*[49]

It is clear from these early paintings that Vanessa was a modernist painter and ahead of her time. She broke new ground with her ideas of form, line and colour. These radical works should have earned her a place in art history. However, she was not ambitious for critical acclaim and, being a woman, she did not receive it. Having made her mark, she moved on. Art historians have overlooked her contribution to the foundation of modern British art. Why? At that period there was no avant-garde tradition in England.

In Vanessa's brief dalliance with abstraction and with the idea of moving art away from the confines of tradition and the fundamental reliance on the art of drawing, as taught at the Slade; the influences of all the artists she had seen in Europe, and the paintings of the two Post-Impressionist exhibitions of Roger Fry, had flooded into her psyche and revealed themselves in her language of paint. Vanessa, Duncan Grant and Roger Fry were no longer 'under the Victorian cloud.' The freshness of approach to painting by Cezanne, Bonnard, Pissarro, Van Gogh, Gauguin, and Matisse was a release for their own inventiveness.

Indeed, this early experimentation in abstraction, though short-lived, was the first wave of modernism before Ben Nicholson's generation. Nicholson, along with other recalcitrant students at the Slade, would have seen the work in Roger Fry's Post-Impressionist exhibitions, especially since these drew the derision of their tutors at the Slade. Ben Nicholson's first abstract painting

Above left: *Vanessa Bell* Abstract Painting *1912*

Above right: *Vanessa Bell*, The Tub *1917*

Right: 1924 (first abstract painting) *by Ben Nicholson.* © Angela Verran Taunt 2014. All rights reserved, DACS

was dated 1924. Vanessa's first abstract painting preceded his by twelve years.

William Rothenstein noted the early signs of Vanessa's rejection of the art of the past masters:

I was asked to make a pastel portrait of Leslie Stephen . . . for Trinity Hall, Cambridge, his old College. Vanessa Stephen was then studying at the Slade School. Pre-Raphaelitism was by now forgotten, and she impressed me, when I met her in houses where the older ideas still lingered, with the quiet courage of her opinions. She looked as though she might have walked among the fair women of Burne-Jones's Golden Stairs; but she spoke with the voice of Gauguin.[50]

In this year of 1913 we see Vanessa turning more and more away from Roger and transferring her affections to Duncan. She prefers to sketch and paint quietly with him, and not engage in intellectual talk and analysis of paintings with Roger. Also she prefers Duncan's work to Roger's. But Duncan is homosexual. She writes to Virginia from Italy where she is travelling with Clive, Roger and Duncan. With regard to the latter she wrote: *My love was not repulsed. I fear it was not even noticed.*[51]

Omega Workshops

Fired by his enthusiasm that had been aroused by mounting the two Post-Impressionist exhibitions, Roger Fry developed the Omega Workshops at 33 Fitzroy Square in 1913, catering for every domestic decorative requirement for the home from pictures, pottery, screens, carpets, furniture, curtains to ladies' fashion.

Vanessa designed dinner and tea sets under the maker's name of Clarice Cliff. They were sold at Harrods and titled 'Modern Art for the Table'. Vanessa's blue floral design was popular. The complete dinner service comprised meat dishes, tureens, jugs, small and large plates, dessert plates, soup bowls, and tea and coffee sets. Every piece was stamped with the artist's signature and maker's name. In spring 2002 the Bloomsbury Workshop reproduced Vanessa's design. The Victoria and Albert Museum has a nearly complete original set of this service.

Ottoline Morrell supported the Omega Workshops by buying hand-printed materials from their showroom. Vanessa Bell and Duncan Grant were part of the management team, with Jessie Etchells, Winifred Gill, Dora Carrington, Barbara Hiles Bagenal, Dorothy Brett and others producing some of the work. There was also a room design for an Ideal Home stand, with geometric patterns and straight lines in Art Deco style. In 1916 Vanessa held her first solo show on the premises at 33 Fitzroy Square.

Modern Art for the table

Meeting Picasso

In 1914 Vanessa, Clive and Roger were taken by Gertrude Stein to meet Picasso in Paris. Vanessa described Picasso as simple and charming. His studio very large and light 'bristling with Picassos.' There were portraits of the blue period, a great many other paintings, and arrangements of coloured papers and bits of wood. Vanessa concluded that he was: *one of the greatest geniuses that has ever lived. His gifts seemed to me simply amazing.*[52] Matisse had only one or two unfinished pieces in his studio. Vanessa was out of France before hostilities began and the first world war closed doors to travel.

In 1915 Vanessa described that winter in London at Gower Street, the home of Ottoline Morrell, the great patroness of the arts:

We spent a very gay winter in London, far gayer than usual. Ottoline took it upon herself to keep us all merry and gave a party every week, at which you might see Bertie Russell dancing a hornpipe, Lytton and Oliver and Marjorie Strachey cutting capers, Duncan dancing in much the same way that he paints, Augustus John and Arnold Bennett and all the celebrities of the day looking as beautiful as they could in clothes seized from Ottoline's drawers, and Ottoline herself at the head of a troupe of short haired young ladies from the Slade prancing about.[53]

In writing to Roger Fry, Vanessa also described Christmas spent at Garsington Manor, Ottoline and Philip's home in Oxford, which became a refuge for a number of conscientious objectors to the war, and their pacifist sympathizers:

There is a large party here - ourselves and the children, Maynard, Lytton, Maria, J M Murray . . then Julian and the Swiss governess . . Ottoline is really amazing – she has all the servants in . . and the dance to which the villagers came was a great success . . there was none of that awful stiffness that generally comes with mixed classes. I suppose it's her aristocratic tradition that makes her able to do it. [54]

In 1915 Duncan painted a rather blowzy portrait of *Vanessa in a Red Dress*, and a similar one in a red dress three years later. They seem indicative of her frame of mind at this time when she was falling in love with Duncan. This is a period when, in order to please him, she goes in for bawdy badinage, and hotly defends buggery, complaining of those people who neither understand buggery nor abstract painting – she appears to put the two on the same level. It strikes one as a desperate appeal to Duncan to love her. In order to attract him, she has a bath in his presence, to which Duncan seemed 'quite unmoved' and 'Clive didn't object.' She offered to pose for Duncan in a series of erotic or indecent studies of copulation, which she suggests Roger could hang in his show. Quentin Bell, in his introduction to *Vanessa Bell's Family Album*, writes 'our views on art, on literature, on religion and, although I did not then know it, on sex, were hopelessly unorthodox.'

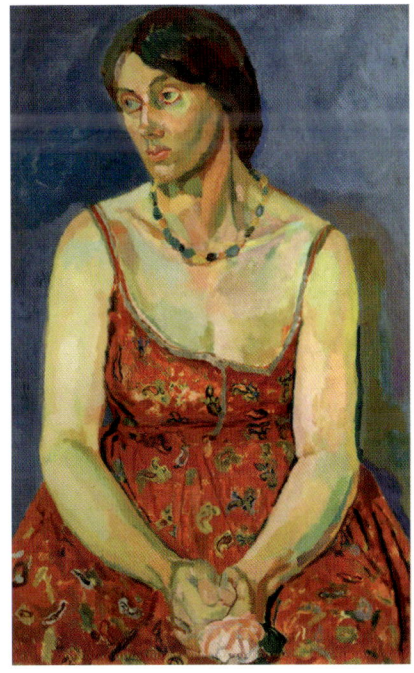

Vanessa in a Red Dress
by Duncan Grant
© National Portrait Gallery

In 1917-18 Vanessa was about to give birth to Angelica, the child by Duncan Grant. She was also working on a painting *The Tub* which characterised the end of a series she had produced up to that time. She also produced a woodcut of *The Tub* in 1919 for the Omega Workshops. A woman stands naked beside a bath of water. The subject of the painting was Mary Hutchinson, Clive Bell's present girl friend, yet it was likened by Angelica, years later, to a self-portrait symbolising loneliness. Vanessa wrote to Roger Fry: *I've been working at my big bath picture and am rather excited about that. I've taken out the woman's chemise and in consequence she is quite nude and much more decent.*[55]

If Angelica Bell is correct that the picture symbolizes loneliness, then perhaps we can attribute this loneliness to the all too brief affair Vanessa had with Duncan Grant, which resulted in the birth of their daughter, Angelica, at Christmas in 1918. Soon after the birth sexual relations ceased between the two, by agreement, but obviously at Duncan's insistence.

Duncan declined to own the child as his. The complicity of the three in claiming Angelica as the child of Clive seems uncharacteristic of people who cared so little for other people's opinions and morality. One can only assume that Duncan did not want to accept the responsibility of being a

Interior with artist's daughter, Angelica Bell, *Vanessa Bell*

father, and to have that title cluttering up his chosen homosexual lifestyle. Vanessa must have been hurt by this double rejection, and certainly, Angelica was upset when the truth was revealed to her at the age of eighteen.

Looking at the work of both Duncan and Vanessa, she is the equal artist, but at the time it was Duncan whose reputation was the greater. Roger Fry's painting is governed by the outlines he uses which restrict his colour and his subject matter. His work therefore is more restrained. Vanessa found difficulty in praising his work. Roger's advice to her was not to paint the same subject matter as Duncan, whether still life or portrait, and therefore invite unfavourable comparison. But Vanessa and Duncan were comfortable painting together. 'We talk of hardly anything but painting.' Indeed, in Fry's exhibition of 1921 *Nameless* in which all the exhibitors were anonymous, Henry Tonks mistook a painting by Vanessa for a Duncan Grant. Vanessa was surprised and flattered, but Tonks compounded his mistake and his prejudice by giving a little lecture on how pitiful it was that women always imitated men.

Charleston and the Later Paintings

During the First World War many of the Bloomsbury men were conscientious objectors, and Vanessa, in order to be with Duncan Grant and to escape from London, rented Charleston farmhouse, near Lewes in East Sussex. Grant, and David Garnett, were required to work on the land, and Vanessa provided a home for them. It was Virginia who had first viewed Charleston and found it admirable. In September 1916 Virginia wrote to Vanessa from Carbis Bay, Cornwall, saying how exciting it was to think of Vanessa and Charleston and if she did get the house 'you'll end up by buying it forever.' Virginia's forecast was to prove true. Vanessa described the house and garden to Roger Fry:

There's a wall of trees – one single line of elms all round two sides . . . We are just below Firle Beacon . . Inside the house the rooms are very large . . Ten bedrooms I think some enormous. One I shall make into a studio. The Omega dinner service looks most lovely in the dresser.[56]

And so began the move to this precious house: furniture, studio materials of paint and canvas, children and servants. Many of the rooms remained empty until Vanessa could fill them with odd and old bits of furniture, which she painted and decorated to fit in with her style of living. In the more settled atmosphere of Charleston and the surrounding countryside Vanessa began to let her small world close in on her. She gradually turned to domestic subjects for her paintings, and lost interest in the explorative elements of abstraction: *Bloomsbury's abstract period was short-lived. In Vanessa's case interest waned because she needed to bring to her art more of her experience of life than the conceptual purity of abstract art allowed.*[57]

Vanessa and Duncan encircled themselves by decorating all the surfaces of the house with patterns and paintings, chairs, lampshades, bed heads, tables and walls. They painted side by side, using the same models and still-life subjects, and remained content to do so for the rest of their lives. Various companies sought the pairs' decorating and design skills.

The dining room
Vanessa Bell and Duncan Grant

Vanessa's Studio

Vanessa's studio at Charleston is described by Angelica Garnett as the sanctuary in which she spent some of the most treasured moments of her childhood. The war caught up with Bloomsbury at last and various friends were dispersed throughout the country. At Charleston the two men, Duncan Grant and David Garnett, worked on the local farm. They were lovers and Vanessa experiences some unhappiness when she feels excluded. However, her love for Duncan allows her to put his happiness before her own and she has to be content that he likes her company. She is also prepared to promote Duncan's painting over her own and writes to Ottoline Morrell to say how pleased she is that Ottoline has persuaded her brother to buy three of Duncan's works, and she offers anything of her own as a gift.

Vanessa's painting *Clive Bell and his Family* is a one-off painting. She writes to Roger:

Grace in the kitchen at Charleston,
Vanessa Bell

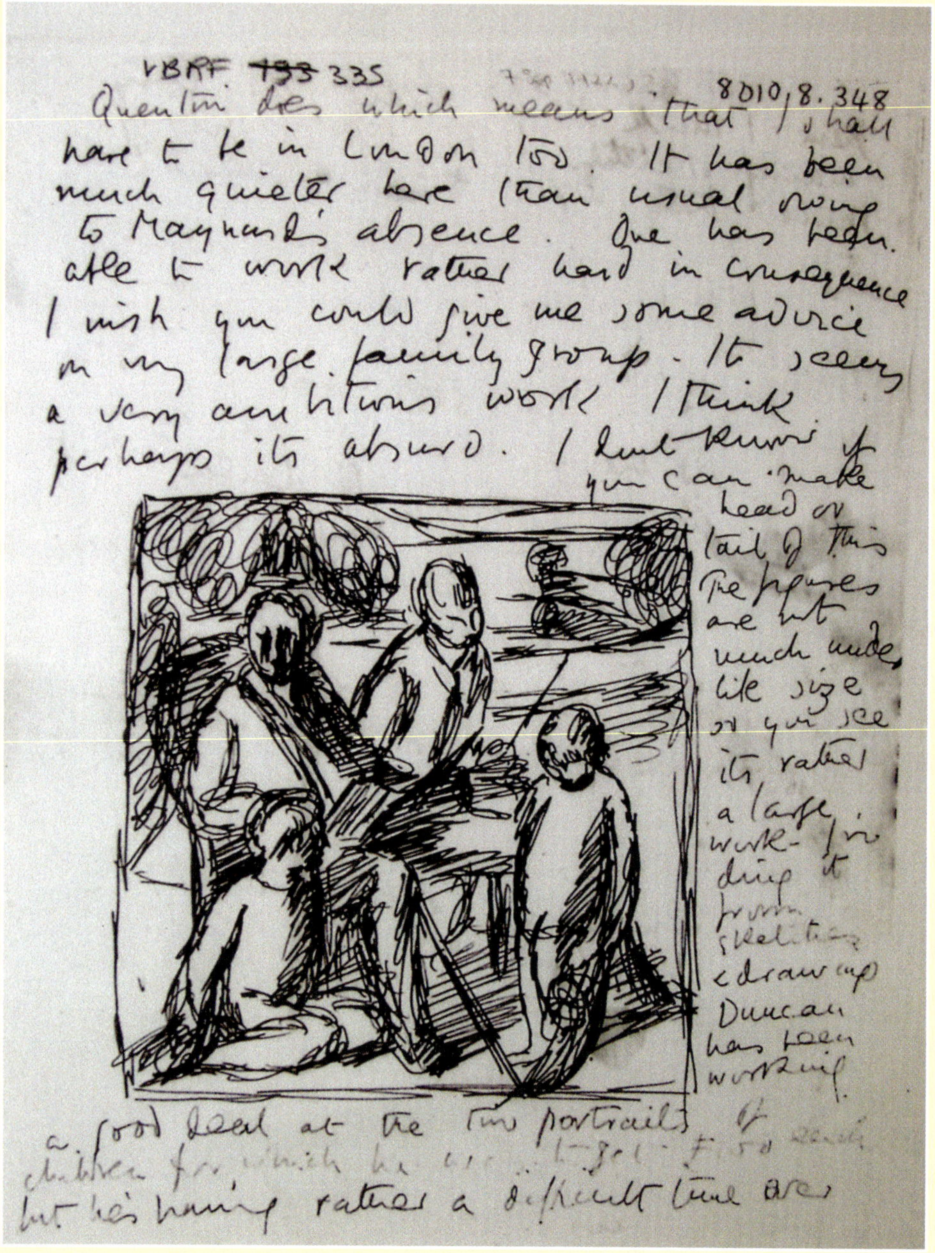

Virginia Woolf & Vanessa Bell - A CHILDHOOD IN ST IVES

> Quentin does which means that I shall have to be in London too. It has been much quieter here than usual owing to Maynard's absence. One has been able to work rather hard in consequence. I wish you could give me some advice on my large family group. It seems a very ambitious work. I think perhaps its absurd. I don't know if you can make head or tail of this. The figures are about much under life size as you see its rather a large work. I'm doing it from skeliting & drawings Duncan has been working a good deal at the two portraits of children for which he uses [...] but he's having rather a difficult time as

Vanessa's family group

I wish you could give me some advice on my large family group. It seems a very ambitious work. I think perhaps it's absurd. I don't know if you can make head or tail of this. The figures are not much under life size so you see it's rather a large work. I'm doing it from sketches and drawings.[58]

This letter to Roger Fry is dated 1922. I think it significant that Vanessa had been to visit Stanley Spencer and watched him painting at the Oratory of All Souls. His work was completed in 1922. One cannot help but notice the likeness to Stanley's chunky figure portraits and feel that Vanessa has incorporated his influence into her work.

Charleston Farmhouse

Charleston Becomes Permanent

In 1939 Vanessa is prepared to settle permanently at Charleston. It is the stable element in her life. Although Virginia is always in love with Cornwall, Vanessa transfers her allegiance to her house in Sussex. It is her staunch, supporting rock on which she relies. Although Vanessa's responsibilities are manifold, with three children, Virginia's continued dependence, Clive Bell's vicissitudes, the heartache of Duncan's love affairs, she maintains a pivotal role in all these lives – and there is always art. And at the heart of Vanessa's life there is Charleston, the house she loves, which contains everyone she loves, and within it is her studio and her paints and canvas.

Vanessa's daughter Angelica Garnett, in her autobiography *Deceived with Kindness*, remarks how her mother was the magnetic centre of the household at Charleston, whether at the dining table, or in her studio:

Vanessa's self portrait

... *Vanessa was self-reliant almost to a fault, producing an effect of rocklike stability that was not as secure as it seemed. For the rest of her life she spent a large part of her energy in creating and maintaining a circle of safety, within which she could gather together all the elements she most loved and depended on. Her mother's early death may well have stimulated a fear of the outside world and a deep need of family life.*[59]

Charleston becomes the memorial for a lifetime of colour. She lovingly decorates, patterns and transforms objects of use to a design for living. Art was doing, not discussing. It was colour, shape and form in a practical world of chosen friends and family. Frances Partridge felt the house gave the impression of having developed spontaneously:

Charleston in its heyday was an enchanted place – a place of such potent individuality that whenever I stayed there I came away grateful to it, as it were, for giving me so much pleasure, so many rich and various visual sensations, such talk, such a sense that lives were being intensely and purposefully led there.[60]

In the spring of 1961 Vanessa died; twenty years after her sister, Virginia. Her life, with all its compromises, was as rewarding as she could have wished. Her dying at home, in her studio, which was also her bedroom and led directly into her garden, was equally appropriate. Charleston is a fitting memorial. Virginia's words in To The Lighthouse quite unintentionally but so very aptly, sums up Vanessa as the artist: *For nothing so solaced her, eased her of the perplexity of life, and miraculously raised its burdens, as this sublime power, this heavenly gift, and one would no more disturb it, while it lasted, than break up the shaft of sunlight lying level across the floor.*[61]

Vanessa's Studio

A Brief Chronology

30th May 1879	Vanessa Stephen born
1880	Thoby Stephen born
1881	Leslie Stephen buys the lease of Talland House
25th January 1882	Virginia Stephen born
1882	The Stephen family spend their first summer at Talland House
1883	Adrian Stephen born
5th May 1895	Death of Julia Stephen. Lease of Talland House sold
Sept. 1901-1904	Vanessa enters the Royal Academy Schools
February 1904	Death of Sir Leslie Stephen
October	Vanessa studies briefly at the Slade School of Art
Aug-Oct 1905	Vanessa, Thoby, Virginia and Adrian stay at Trevose View, Carbis Bay. Visit the Thomas, Millie Dow family at Talland House
February 7th 1907	Vanessa Stephen marries Clive Bell
April 1908	Virginia, Vanessa, Clive with baby Julian stay at Trevose House Draycott Terrace, St Ives
Xmas 1909	Virginia stays on her own at the Lelant Hotel (now Badger Inn)
March 1910	Virginia, Clive and Vanessa stay at Lelant
Aug-Sept	Virginia on walking tour with Jean Thomas. Stay at Porthmeor Farm near Gurnard's Head and at Lelant
November 1910	Opening of Roger Fry's First Post-Impressionist Exhibition
Aug 10th 1912	Virginia marries Leonard Woolf Vanessa sells her first painting to the Contemporary Art Society
October 1912	Vanessa shows in Roger Fry's second Post-Impressionist show
April 1914	Virginia and Leonard visit St Ives and stay at the Carbis Bay Hotel
1915	*The Voyage Out* Virginia's first novel, published by Duckworth
September 1916	Virginia and Leonard stay with Margaret Llewelyn Davies at Gwel Martin in Carbis Bay
October 1916	Vanessa moves to Charleston
1917	Two Stories first publication of the Hogarth Press
March 1921	Virginia and Leonard stay at Poniou and with the Arnold Forsters at Eagle's Nest, Zennor
Xmas 1926	Virginia and Leonard stay at Eagle's Nest with the Arnold Forsters
1927	*To the Lighthouse* published
1936	Virginia and Leonard stay at Eagle's Nest with the Arnold Forsters
1940	Vanessa's early paintings destroyed by bomb on Fitzroy Street Studio
28th March 1941	Virginia Woolf commits suicide by drowning in the River Ouse
7th April 1961	Vanessa Bell dies at Charleston

Notes and References

Abbreviations

CD   Collected Diaries. *The Diary of Virginia Woolf,* vols 1-5 ed. Anne Olivier Bell (Penguin, London 1985)
CL   Virginia Woolf, *The Collected Letters*, vols I-VI, eds. Nigel Nicolson and Joanne Trautmann (Harcourt Brace Jovanovich, New York 1975-1980)
MB   Leslie Stephen, *Mausoleum Book,* ed. Alan Bell (OUP, Oxford 1977)
MoB   Virginia Woolf, *Moments of Being,* ed. Jeanne Schulkind (Harcourt Brace, New York 1985)
PA   Virginia Woolf, *A Passionate Apprentice: The Early Journals 1897-1909,* ed. Mitchell Leaska (Harvest/HBJ, USA 1992)
SP&I Vanessa Bell, *Sketches in Pen & Ink,* ed. Lia Giachero, (Pimlico, London 1998)
LLLS *Life & Letters of Leslie Stephen*, ed. F.W. Maitland, (Duckworth & Company, London 1906)
SLLS *Selected Letters of Leslie Stephen,* ed. F.W. Bicknell, (Macmillan, London 1996)
TL   Virginia Woolf, *To the Lighthouse,* (Vintage, London 1992)
SLVB *Selected Letters of Vanessa Bell,* ed. Regina Marler, (Bloomsbury, London 1993)
CB   Clive Bell
JS   Julia Stephen
LS   Leslie Stephen
LW   Leonard Woolf
SDS   Stella Duckworth Stephen
VB   Vanessa Bell
VS   Virginia Stephen
VW   Virginia Woolf

Notes

Part 1: AN INTRODUCTION TO ST IVES
1   Virginia Woolf, *MoB*, p.129
2   *SDS*, 1893
3   *SDS*, 1893
4   *St Ives Heritage,* Lena & Donald Bray, Cornwall 1981)
5   *SDS*, 1893
6   *Historical Sketch of St Ives & District,* Badcock, St Ives 1896)
7   *A Painters' Club,* Louis Grier, The Studio 1900
8   *St Ives Times, Christmas Number, 1925* Julius Olsson
9   *Western Echo,* February 1904

Part 2: VIRGINIA WOOLF
1   Reminiscences, MoB p.128
2   MoB p.128
3   VW Diary, March 1921 Vol.2
4   In conversation with Marion Whybrow 1993
5   LLLS p.349 Duckworth 1906
6   SLLS Vol.2, p. 297-99
7   Ibid p.298
8   HPGN August 1892
9   Granite & Rainbow, Mitchell Leaska, p.49 Hogarth Press 1958

NOTES AND REFERENCES

10 H M Swanwick, *I Have Been Young* p.107, Gollancz, London 1935
11 Granite & Rainbow, Mitchell Leaska, p.51, Hogarth Press 1958
12 SLLS 1883 p.361
13 SDS Diary 1893
14 MoB, p.133
15 SLLS Vol.2, p.369
16 HPGN June 1892
17 The Spectator, RA Summer Exhibition 1890
18 MoB, p.132
19 Life and Letters of Sir Edmund Gosse, Wm Heinemann 1931
20 SDS Diary 1893
21 HPGN August 1892
21a *Daily Mail, 1908, Charles Marriott*
21b LW *Downhill All the Way* p.153
22 Donald & Lena Bray, *St Ives Heritage*
23 MoB p.144
24 PA April p.64/65
25 HPGN 1892
26 PA February 1897 p.34
27 PA July 1903, p.176
27a PA March 1905, p.245
28 PA April 1905, p.268
29 In conversation with Marion Whybrow 1993
30 SLVB, April 1908, p.62-63
31 Letters of Virginia Woolf, September-October, 1905
32 VS to VB Christmas Day 1909
33 MoB p.198
34 SLVB, May 1927, p.317
35 Ibid, May 1927, p.318
36 Sowing – An Autobiography of the Years 1800-1904. Leonard Woolf, New York 1988
37 Diary of Virginia Woolf, Vol.1, March 1918
38 D H Lawrence Selected Letters; Tinners Arms, Zennor p101
39 Katherine Mansfield Letters & Journals, p.132/3 Penguin Modern Classics, 1977
40/40a A Boy at the Hogarth Press, Richard Kennedy. Heinemann 1972
41/42 Katherine Mansfield Letters & Journals, p.132/3 Penguin Modern Classics, 1977
43/44/45 Carrington, Letters & Extracts from her Diaries, p.242,261 Jonathan Cape, 1970

Part 3: VANESSA BELL
1 *SP&I*, p.63
2 *LLLS*, p.336
3 *Ibid*, p.345
4 *SLLS*, Vol.2, p304
5 *Ibid*, p.305
6 Virginia Woolf, *MoB*, p.34
7 SDS, 1893
8 Vanessa Bell, Frances Spalding, (Weidenfeld & Nicholson, London 1994), p.ll
9 *St Ives 1883-1993 Portrait of an Art Colony*, Marion Whybrow p.39
10 Virginia Woolf, *MoB*, p.128
11 SDS, 1893

12 *Days in Cornwall,* Charles Lewis Hind (Methuen & Co. London 1907
13 SDS, 1893
14 *St Ives Weekly Summary,* 1895
15 Virginia Woolf, *Walter Sickert: A Conversation,* The Hogarth Press, London 1934) p.17
16 *A Painters' Club,* Louis Grier, (The Studio Magazine, 1895)
17 Virginia Woolf, *PA,* January 1897, p.7
18 *SLVB,* January 1905, p.29
19 Virginia Woolf, PA, March 1905, p.246
20 *SLVB,* March 1916, p.192-194
21 *St Ives Weekly Summary,* 1896
22 *SLVB* February 1901, p.7
23 *The Magazine of Art,* 1890, p.642
24 *SLLS,* p.527
25 *SLLS,* Vol.l, p.213
26 Virginia Woolf, *PA,* p.16
27 Original Letter from Vanessa Bell to Margery Snowden, undated, (Tate London)
28 Ibid
29 *SP&I,* p.118
30 Ibid, p.98
31 *An Unfinished Autobiography,* H A L Fisher, (OUP 1940)
32 SDS, 1897
33 *SP&I,* p.73
34 *SP&I,* p.81
35 Original Letter from VB to Margery Snowden, Trevose View, Carbis Bay, 1905 (Tate Gallery, London)
36 Vanessa Bell, Frances Spalding, (Weidenfeld & Nicholson, London 1994) p.125
37 Original Letter from VB to Margery Snowden, Trevose View, Carbis Bay 1905 (Tate Gallery, London)
38 *SP&I,* (Lecture at Leighton Park School) p.157
39 Original Letter from VB to Margery Snowden (Tate Gallery, London)
40 Ibid
41 *SLVB,* March 1909, P.80
42 *Ibid,* April 1908, p.61
43 *The Art of Bloomsbury,* Richard Shone, (Tate Gallery Catalogue of Exhibition 1999)
44 *SP&I,* p.126
45 *Ibid,* p.129
46 Leonard Woolf, *Beginning Again, An Autobiography* 1911-1918, (Hogarth Press, London1964) p.93-96
47 *SLVB,* August 1912, p.122
48 *Ibid,* p.126
49 *The Art of Bloomsbury,* Richard Shone, (Tate Gallery Catalogue of Exhibition 1999)
50 *Men & Memories,* Wm. Rothenstein, Vol.2 (Faber & Faber, London) p.53
51 *SLVB,* January 1918, p.209
52 *Ibid,* May 1913, p.l39
53 Vanessa Bell, Francis Spalding, p125 (Weidenfeld & Nicholson, London 1994)
54 Original Letter from VB to Roger Fry, Xmas 1915 (Tate Gallery, London)
55 Letter to Roger Fry
56 Letter to Roger Fry
57 *Deceived with Kindness,* Angelica Garnett, (Chatto & Windus, Hogarth Press 1984, London) p.23
58 *Memories,* Frances Partridge, (Phoenix, London 1996) p.163
59 *To The Lighthouse,* (Vintage, London 1992) p.44

Select Bibliography

Badcock W *Historical Sketch of St Ives& District 1896* W Badcock, St Ives

Bell, Quentin *Virginia Woolf* Pimlico, London 1996

Bell, Vanessa *Selected Letters* ed Regina Marler. Moyer Bell, Rhode Island 1998

Bray, Donald & Lena *St Ives Heritage, Recollections and Records of St Ives, Carbis Bay and Lelant.* Dyllansow Truran, Cornwall 1981

Caws, Mary Ann *Women of Bloomsbury: Vanessa, Virginia and Carrington.* Routledge, London 1990

Curtis, Vanessa *Virginia Woolf's Women.* Robert Hale, London 2002

Dunn, Jane *A Very Close Conspiracy, Virginia Woolf and Vanessa Bell.* Pimlico, London 1995

Fisher H A L *An Unfinished Autobiography.* OUP, Oxford 1940

Fry, Roger *Letters of Roger Fry vols. 1 & 2 1878-1934*, Ed Denys Sutton. Chatto & Windus, London 1972

Garnett, Angelica *Deceived With Kindness.* Chatto & Windus, Hogarth Press, London 1984

Garnett, Angelica *Vanessa Bell's Family Album.* Norman and Hobhouse, London 1981

Garnett, David *Carrington, Letters and Extracts from her Diaries.* OUP, Oxford 1979

Gayford, Martin *Still Winding and Wonderful: Zennor's Literary and Artistic Connections.* Charleston Magazine No 19, Charleston Trust

Giachero, Lia (ed) *Vanessa Bell: Sketches in Pen and Ink.* Pimlico, London 1998

Gillespie, D F *The Sisters' Arts.* Syracuse University Press, New York 1991

Hepworth, Barbara *A Pictorial Autobiography.* Moonraker Press, Wiltshire 1978

Hill, Jane *The Art of Dora Carrington.* The Herbert Press, London 1994

Hill-Miller, Katherine *From the Lighthouse to Monk's House.* Duckworth, London 2001

Hind, Charles, Lewis *Days in Cornwall.* Methuan & Co. London 1907

Jacobs, Michael *The Good & Simple Life.* Phaidon, London 1985

Kennedy, Richard *A Boy at the Hogarth Press.* Whittington Press, London 1972

Lawrence D H *Selected Letters.* Penguin Books 1950

Leaska, Mitchell (ed) *A Passionate Apprentice. The Early Journals. Virginia Woolf 1897-1909.* The Hogarth Press, London 1990

Leaska, Mitchell *Granite and Rainbow.* Hogarth Press, London 1958

Lee, Hermione *Virginia Woolf.* Vintage, London 1997

Maitland F W *The Life and Letters of Leslie Stephen.* Duckworth & Co. London 1906

Mansfield, Katherine *Letters and Journals.* Penguin Book 1977

Marsh, Jan *Bloomsbury Women. Distinct Pictures in Life & Art.* Pavilion Books, London 1995

Naylor, Gillian *Bloomsbury. The Artists, Authors & Designers by Themselves.* Pyramid Books, London 1990

Nicholson, Virginia *An Artist's Home, Charleston.* The Charleston Trust 1999

Noall, Cyril *The Book of St Ives.* Friends of St Ives Library 2000

Partridge, Frances *Memories.* Phoenix, London 1981

Raymont, Morton C *Memories of Old St Ives.* St Ives Times 1958

Rothenstein, William *Men and Memories.* Vol.2. Faber and Faber, London 1934

Shone, Richard *Bloomsbury Portraits. Vanessa Bell, Duncan Grant and Their Circle.* Phaideon Press, London 1993

Shone, Richard *The Art of Bloomsbury.* Tate Gallery Publishing, London 1999

Shulkind, Jeanne (ed) *Virginia Woolf – Moments of Being.* Harcourt Brace N.Y. 1985

Spalding, Frances *Vanessa Bell.* Weidenfeld and Nicholson, London 1994

Stephen, Leslie *Selected Letters of Leslie Stephen, vols. 1 & 2* 1864-1904 ed John Bicknell. Macmillan, London 1996

Stephen, Leslie *Mausoleum Book,* ed Alan Bell. Clarendon Press, Oxford 1977

Swanwick, Helena *I Have Been Young.* Gollancz, London 1935 Tabb House, Padstow, Cornwall 1992

Thomas, Charles *'To the Lighthouse' The Story of Godrevy Light.* Penwith Books, Redruth, Cornwall 1985

Tomaline, Claire *Katherine Mansfield, A Secret Life.* Penguin, London 1988

Tovey, David St Ives Art-1890 – The Dawn of the Colony

    Creating a Splash – The St Ives Society of Artists 1927-1952

    St Ives (1860-1930) The Artists & the Community – A Social History

Whybrow, Marion *Borlase Smart, St Ives Artist, Man of Vision.* Halsgrove Books, Somerset 2012

Whybrow, Marion *St Ives : The Story of Porthmeor Studios.* Halsgrove, 2013

Whybrow, Marion *St Ives 1883-1993 Portrait of an Art Colony.* Antique Collectors' Club, Woodbridge, 1994, Reprinted by Harbour Bookshop, St Ives 2002

Whybrow, Marion *Leach Pottery, St Ives, The Legacy of Bernard Leach.* Beach Books, St Ives, Cornwall 2006

Woolf, Leonard *Beginning Again. An Autobiography 1911-1918.* Hogarth Press, London 1964

Woolf, Leonard *Downhill All the Way. An Autobiography of the Years 1919-1939.* Harcourt Brace Jovanovich, New York 1975

Woolf, Leonard *A Writer's Diary* 1953

Woolf, Virginia *The Diary of Virginia Woolf,* vols. 1-5, ed Anne Olivier Bell. Penguin, London 1985

Woolf, Virginia *The Collected Letters,* vols.1-V1, ed Nigel Nicholson and Joanne Trautmann. Harcourt Brace Jovanovich, New York, 1975-1980

Woolf, Virginia *To the Lighthouse.* Vintage, London 1992

Woolf, Virginia *Moments of Being* Triad/Granada 1978

Index

Arts Club (St Ives) 7, 27, 28, 34, 38, 49, 50, 52, 53, 65, 94

Bartlett, W H 51, 106
Bell, Angelica 57, 115, 116, 117, 119,
Bell, Clive 59, 61, 66, 103, 106, 107, 110, 113, 114, 115, 117, 119, 121
Bell, Julian 59, 61, 107, 110, 115, 121
Bell, Quentin 57, 63, 109, 110, 115
Bell, Vanessa 7, 8, 10, 12, 13, 14, 16, 18, 20, 22, 24, 26, 28, 30, 32, 33, 34, 35, 36, 37, 38, 40, 42, 44, 46, 48, 49, 50, 52, 53, 54, 56, 57, 58, 59, 60, 61, 62, 63, 64, 65, 66, 67, 68, 69, 70, 71, 72, 74, 76, 78, 79, 83, 84, 86, 87, 89, 90, 91, 93, 94, 95, 96, 97, 98, 99, 101, 102, 103, 104, 106, 107, 109, 110, 111, 113, 114, 115, 116, 117, 118, 119, 120, 121
Birch, Lamorna 87
Bloomsbury 8, 52, 57, 59, 65, 68, 93, 103, 110, 113, 116, 117
Bolitho, Bedford MP 51
Bonnard, Pierre 111
Brangwyn, Frank 99
Bray, Donald 4, 53
Brenan, Gerald 78
Brett, Dorothy 98, 113

Brooke, Rupert 102
Brown, Ford Madox 95
Brown, Frederick 97, 98, 106, 110
Burne Jones, Edward 52

Cameron, Julia Margaret 57
Carbis Bay 17, 33, 61, 66, 80, 116, 121
Carrington, Dora 68, 78, 97, 98, 113
Cave Day, William 28
Cezanne, Paul 109, 111
Charleston 116, 117, 119, 120, 121
Cliff, Clarice 113
Compton Mackenzie, Fay 52
Cox, Ka 65, 98

Detmold, Henry 106
Dow, Florence Millie 55
Dow, Thomas Millie 55, 90, 106
Duckworth, George 35
Duckworth, Gerald 33, 57
Duckworth, Stella 25, 51, 57
Dunmore, Helen 7, 8

Eagle's Nest 38, 65, 66, 75, 121
Etchells, Jessie 113

Falmouth 87, 106

Fauvists 111
Forbes, Elizabeth 89, 94
Forbes, Stanhope 7, 27, 102
Forster, Arnold 38, 65
Forster, E M 52, 71
Forster, Katherine 38. 65, 121
Forster, Morgan 66, 71
Freeman, William 20
Fry, Roger 66, 109, 110, 111, 113, 115, 116, 119, 121
Fuller, Leonard 82, 98

Garnett, David 66, 116, 117
Gertler, Mark 94, 97, 98
Godrevy 15, 16, 20, 42, 48, 53, 54, 71
Gosse, Edmund 51
Gotch, Thomas 106
Grant, Duncan 66, 106, 107, 110, 111, 113, 115, 116, 117
Grier, Louis 7, 27, 28, 29, 84, 85, 86, 91, 94
Gurnard's Head 33, 43, 62, 63, 64, 121

Hain, Edward 12, 24, 26
Hamada, Shoji 99
Hamnett, Nina 98
Harewood, Robinson 127
Hiles, Barbara 98, 113
Hind, Lewis 86
Hogarth Press 4, 68, 69, 71, 76, 121

Hunt, William Holman 52, 95

James, Henry 34, 51
John, Augustus 109, 111, 114
John, Gwen 98, 109

Kennedy, Richard 76, 78
Keynes, John Maynard 66
Knights, Winifred 98

Laidlay, W J 106
Land's End 13, 24, 42, 45, 76
Lanham, James 49, 83, 99
Lanhams 38, 39
Lawrence, D H 68, 74
Lawrence, Frieda 74, 75, 76
Leach, Bernard 99, 101
Lever, Hayley 86, 104, 105
Lindner, Augusta 97
Lindner, Moffat 97, 98, 106
Lowell, James Russell 34

MacCarthy, Desmond 66
Maitland, Frederick 32
Mansfield, Katherine 68, 71, 74, 75, 78, 109
Marriott, Charles 52,

111
Marshall, Frances 68
Matisse, Henri 109, 110, 111, 114
Meredith, George 34, 52
Milais, John Everett 52
Milman, Sylvia Frances 98
Monks House 127
Morrell, Ottoline 68, 94, 113, 114, 117
Morris, William 56, 103
Mortimer, Laurence Sydney 127
Mostyn, Marjorie 98
Murry, John Middleton 74

Nash, Paul 97
Newlyn 7, 19, 26, 27, 87, 89, 90, 98, 102, 106
Nicholson, Ben 97, 101, 111, 112
Norton, Charles Eliot 49, 79

Olsson, Julius 27, 29, 59, 91, 92, 97, 106

Park, John 104, 105
Partridge, Ralph 68, 78
Picasso, Pablo 109, 110, 114
Pissarro, Camille 111
Porthminster Beach 7, 12, 16, 17, 18, 19, 37, 38, 46, 47, 48, 49, 52, 60, 97, 102, 107

127

Porthmeor 20, 63, 65, 86, 87, 91, 121
Pre-Raphaelites 52, 95
Procter, Dod 98

Ragamice 46, 47
Richthofen, Baron Von 76
Robinson, Maria 28, 84
Rodin, Auguste 103
Rothenstein, William 113
Royal Academy 31, 50, 58, 59, 87, 89, 91, 94, 95, 96, 97, 101, 106, 121

Sargent, John Singer 101, 106
Schjerfbeck, Helene 7, 87, 89
Shone, Richard 4, 107
Sickert, Walter 26, 47, 71, 93, 94, 109
Simmons, Edward E 50
Simmons, Vesta 49
Simpson, Ruth 29
Slade School of Art 4, 59, 94, 97, 98, 99, 101, 110, 111, 113, 114, 121
Sloop Inn 32
Smart, Borlase 22, 26, 27, 45, 66, 92, 93
Smith, George 40
Snowden, Margery 58, 96, 109
Spencer, Stanley 97, 98, 110, 119
Steer, Philip Wilson 97
Stein, Gertrude 114
Stephen, Adrian 121
Stephen, Julia 13, 17, 26, 40, 50, 51, 53, 94, 95, 121
Stephen, Leslie 7, 10, 26, 27, 29, 31, 32, 34, 43, 44, 49, 50, 51, 52, 69, 79, 96, 103, 113, 121
Stephen, Thoby 44
Stephen, Vanessa 35, 44, 50, 52, 79, 113, 121
Stephen, Virginia 7, 33, 121
Stokes, Adrian 7, 49, 50, 106
Stokes, Marianne 49, 50, 87, 106
Strachey, Lytton 59, 66, 78, 107, 110, 111
Symonds, John Addington 34
Symons, Alison 56

Talland House 7, 8, 12, 13, 15, 20, 26, 29, 33, 34, 35, 37, 42, 46, 47, 48, 49, 51, 52, 53, 54, 55, 56, 57, 59, 69, 71, 79, 84, 87, 91, 95, 97, 101, 102, 121
Talmage, Algernon 29, 59
Thackeray, Laura Minny 35
Titcomb, W H Y 29, 31, 87, 89, 90, 106
Tonks, Henry 97, 98, 99, 101, 110, 116
Towednack 24, 42
Tree, Iris 98
Tregenna Castle Hotel 51
Treloyhan Manor 24, 25, 28, 48
Tuke, Henry Scott 106
Turner, J M W 26

Van Gogh, Vincent 109, 111

Walker, Ethel 98
Wallis, Alfred 20, 21, 100, 101
Walpole, Hugh 52
Watts, George Frederick 52
Westlake, Arnold 43
Whistler, James McNeill 26, 83, 93, 94, 104
Wood, Christopher 101
Woolf, Leonard 33, 65, 66, 68, 69, 110, 121
Woolf, Virginia 7, 8, 10, 12, 14, 16, 18, 20, 22, 24, 26, 28, 30, 32, 33, 34, 35, 36, 37, 38, 39, 40, 41, 42, 43, 44, 45, 46, 47, 48, 49, 50, 51, 52, 53, 54, 55, 56, 57, 58, 59, 60, 61, 62, 63, 64, 65, 66, 67, 68, 69, 70, 71, 72, 73, 74, 75, 76, 77, 78, 80, 81, 82, 84, 86, 88, 90, 92, 94, 96, 98, 100, 102, 104, 106, 108, 110, 111, 112, 114, 116, 118, 120, 121

Zennor 24, 33, 37, 38, 43, 74, 76, 80, 121